Presented To:

_____

From:

_____

Date:

_____

THE ART OF

LEARNING

& SELF-DEVELOPMENT

THE ART OF
LEARNING
& SELF-DEVELOPMENT

YOUR **COMPETITIVE** EDGE

JIM STOVALL
& RAY H. HULL, PhD

SOUND WISDOM
P.O. Box 310
Shippensburg, PA 17257-0310

For more information on publishing and distribution rights, call 717-530-2122 or info@soundwisdom.com

Quantity Sales. Special discounts are available on quantity purchases by corporations, associations, and others. For details, contact the Sales Department at Sound Wisdom.

While efforts have been made to verify information contained in this publication, neither the author nor the publisher assumes any responsibility for errors, inaccuracies, or omissions.

While this publication is chock-full of useful, practical information; it is not intended to be legal or accounting advice. All readers are advised to seek competent lawyers and accountants to follow laws and regulations that may apply to specific situations.

The reader of this publication assumes responsibility for the use of the information. The author and publisher assume no responsibility or liability whatsoever on the behalf of the reader of this publication.

Cover design by Eileen Rockwell
Interior design by Terry Clifton

ISBN 13 HC: 978-1-937879-81-5
ISBN 13 eBook: 978-1-937879-82-2
ISBN 13 TP: 978-1-937879-83-9

For Worldwide Distribution, Printed in the U.S.A.
2 3 4 5 6 7 8 / 20

CONTENTS

CHAPTER ONE

LEARNING ABOUT LEARNING

JIM STOVALL

This book is definitely different from any of the previous 40 titles I've written, and it is quite probably very different from anything you've ever read. Virtually all nonfiction books are about learning something. This book is about learning itself.

Everything known by us as individuals or us collectively as a society has been learned; therefore, we can say all knowledge is a result of learning, but there is very little knowledge about learning. If we were to divide everything we have learned throughout our lives into two basic categories, these categories would be things we have learned through our formal education and things we have learned informally.

This book is similarly divided as I have written the odd-numbered chapters, and my esteemed coauthor Dr. Raymond Hull has written the even chapters. I am very pleased and privileged to, once again, be collaborating with Dr. Hull. We were introduced by a friend and colleague at the U.S. Department of Education, Jo Ann McCann. Our work seems totally dissimilar at first glance but meshes beautifully upon further examination. Our previous coauthored titles include *The Art of Communication* and *The Art of Presentation*. While communication and presentation were complex and broad topics to reduce to writing, they pale in comparison to the vague and mysterious concept of learning.

If we look at the prospect of formal learning, few people anywhere have had more experience as a student or a teacher than Dr. Hull. A brief glance at his credentials listed in this book will attest to his experience and expertise in formal learning. I on the other hand, while proud of my college degree and university education, have learned most of what I know and share through my books, movies, syndicated columns, and speeches informally through a process we commonly refer to as life.

Much learning comes from making mistakes and then becoming aware of how to overcome the same pitfall in the future. Mature learning can come from mistakes made by others and communicated to us directly or through our formal education. Some people can simply read about how long it takes paint to dry and then be empowered to avoid wet paint. Other people must be told by the painter to not touch the wet paint, and some of us don't get the message until we touch the wall and find our hand covered in wet paint. However we come by information and internalize it, learning is the process that elevates us all.

If you want to get ahead in life and pursue what might be called success, there will inevitably be a great deal of learning required no matter what field of endeavor you might pursue. Similarly, we as a society emerged from the stone age and enjoy many modern miracles because of our combined and collective learning.

Formal education allows us to begin our practical learning as we stand on the shoulders of those who have gone before us. Then we are equipped to launch out into our life's work with knowledge gained from previous generations.

As an entrepreneur myself, I often write and give speeches about business. The whole world seems to be looking for one of those quantum leap ideas that can change the world and give them personal and financial success. The only thing required to have a great idea is to go through your daily routine, wait for something bad to happen, and ask yourself one simple question: *How could I have avoided that?* The answer to that question is invariably a great idea. The only thing required to turn your great idea you have learned experientially into a great business is to ask yourself one further question: *How could I help other people avoid that problem?*

All great improvement, development, and success comes from solving problems and helping others to solve their problems. Problem solving is the end result of learning, and learning in the practical world comes from problem solving.

When we learn something, we can change our lives. When we teach someone what we have learned, we can change their lives. But when we teach people to teach, we can change the whole world.

One of the most vital activities in both your formal and informal education is learning through reading. If you were to examine the upward spiral of human development and progress throughout history, you would find that the advent of reading and the emergence of

Gutenberg's printing press caused a great acceleration in human enlightenment.

In our formal education, a huge milestone comes when we learn to read. Much of our early training and learning is directed toward this goal of learning to read. Once we have mastered the skill of reading, we are no longer learning to read but spend the rest of our lives reading to learn.

A great friend, mentor, and publisher of my first novel Charlie "Tremendous" Jones was fond of saying, "You will be the same person you are today five years from now except for the people you meet and the books you read." Charlie was a voracious reader of biographies, which he believed to be simply another way of meeting more people.

As a young boy, I remember a local TV show in my hometown that was hosted by a bookstore owner named Lewis Meyer. Each week Mr. Meyer would review several books and highlight others that were just coming into the market. He would end each program with his motto: "The more books your read, the taller you grow." Mr. Meyer continued to run his independent bookstore long past the age most people retire. I was pleased and honored when my first book came out and he featured it in his bookstore.

If you will think back in your life about the handful of people who have been influential, you will likely discover that one or more of these influencers sparked a love or interest in reading in your life.

As a bestselling author of over 40 books, seven of which have been turned into movies, I am almost embarrassed to share with you, my readers, that when I could read books with my eyes as you are doing at this moment, I rarely read a whole book cover to cover. As a totally blind person for the last quarter of a century, thanks to high-speed listening of audiobooks I am pleased to report that I average reading one book each day. Becoming a reader has made me a writer and brought so many other things into my life, because reading is a foundation of learning.

Traditionally, blind people like me or those with other barriers to the formal educational process were said to have a learning disability. In recent years, new research has emerged along with growing accessibility to education so that now an individual is said to have a learning difference. This is an important development in our society and, quite possibly, in your life.

Gone are the days when we all had to learn the same thing in the same way at the same time. In the twenty-first century, whether you learn formally or informally, traditionally or nontraditionally, ahead or behind of people your age, it is only important that you learn.

Curiosity is one of the most important components of our informal learning. There has never been a better time to be alive for those of us who have an insatiable curiosity and desire to learn than today. The Internet gives us instant access to collective knowledge. While it's important to realize that nothing on the Internet can be taken as an absolute fact, it is a great starting point for learning.

In generations past, if you wanted to know the lifespan of a fruit fly, who played shortstop on the 1946 Yankees, or the length of the coastline of Alaska, you would have to spend several hours in the local library. Today, you simply need to utilize a device that is probably only a few feet away from you as you read these words.

Today, there is almost no excuse for being ignorant of any fact or information, but having access to information and even retaining it in our memory does not mean we have learned it. To complete the cycle of learning, we must master the information and be able to apply it in the real world. Information can be learned and applied incorrectly, which can create a counterproductive or even a dangerous situation.

Shortly after losing my sight, I received training in how to use a white cane to aid me in walking and navigating. One of my favorite destinations was a park near my house. I remember sitting on a bench one day enjoying the sunshine and fresh air when a father walked into the park with his kindergarten-aged son who was struggling with a young puppy straining at its leash.

I could clearly overhear the father explaining how they were going to begin training the dog to obey commands such as come, sit, and stay. At his father's direction, the young boy released the puppy from the leash at which point it proceeded to run with reckless abandon throughout the entire park. The father loudly called for the dog to come, but it ignored his commands for quite some time until eventually the dog, near exhaustion, returned to the father and son and plopped down onto the ground in front of them. The father immediately took a rolled-up newspaper and began to hit the dog. This caused the young boy to burst into tears.

Finally, the father turned to the son and asked, "Do you understand what we're teaching the dog?"

The young boy responded through his tears, saying, "Yes, I understand that the dog has learned when he obeys your command and comes, you will hit him."

The old proverb is true that out of the mouths of babes can come great wisdom. Obviously, the father was not conveying the lesson he intended to teach either his son or the dog.

We must learn the difference between knowledge and wisdom. Simply learning facts does not mean we understand them, and even if we understand them we must apply them if we are to benefit from the learning process.

If someone came into my office and informed me that the building was on fire, they have conveyed some information. If I hear their information and am able to process it and internalize it, I am now aware of the information; however, if I continue to sit in my office as the fire rages around me, it would be hard to say that any learning had taken place.

Part of the ongoing learning process is becoming aware of things we have learned that must be relearned, recalibrated, or applied in new ways.

In one of my previous books, *The Millionaire Map*, I outline my own journey from poverty to prosperity as well as the journey of other wealthy and successful individuals. As a part of that book project, I developed an online Millionaire Profile that readers can take in order to get their own millionaire assessment: www.TheMillionaireMap.com.

One of the key components to this millionaire assessment is a question dealing with original impressions and beliefs about millionaires. I believe that the greatest barriers to wealth and success are mental barriers, so until we can overcome facts we may have learned that simply aren't true we will be held back by this false learning.

Many people believe that millionaires mostly inherit their money and are big winners in the gene-pool lottery. In reality, the facts reveal that approximately 90 percent of millionaires are first generation and earn their money through means and avenues that are available to most of us.

Many people believe the old myth that you have to have money to make money. Once again, the statistics show that most entrepreneurial ventures that result in people becoming millionaires begin with little or no capital. Many people believe that millionaires are greedy and dishonest. The statistics show that millionaires are as generous as the rest of the population, and the vast majority of millionaires play by the rules and have great integrity.

If you are one of the many individuals who have false impressions about millionaires, you have to understand that in order to succeed, you must relearn and apply the new knowledge in the form of wisdom in order to succeed. This is not only important if you want to succeed financially but in every field of endeavor.

False learning or learning that which is not true is counterproductive and dangerous. Much bigotry and prejudice springs from this type of false learning. Anything you learn in your formal education must be demonstrable and repeatable in the real world.

There was a time when the very best learning resulted in people believing that the world was flat and the sun revolved around the earth. In order for the scientific community to progress and move ahead, those facts had to be relearned and applied in the form of new knowledge on which we can continue to build the realm of understanding.

Given the pace of technological advancement today, we must constantly question that which we have learned because a formal education a decade old may be obsolete or even false.

While I am convinced that a formal education can provide an important cornerstone to the value of learning, one of the dangers arises when we graduate. Too many people assume that graduation marks the end of education. While it may be the end of our formal education, it is the beginning of our lifelong education. Life itself is the greatest teacher we can ever have. A graduation ceremony is called a commencement. I believe it signals the beginning or commencing of our real-world, informal learning adventure.

My grandfather only had an eighth-grade education, which during his time was an above-average formal education, but he was one of the most knowledgeable people I ever knew. He constantly read from one of the many volumes of encyclopedias he kept on a shelf near his favorite chair.

My grandfather did not use the encyclopedia like most people did as a reference tool. He started with the first entry in the A volume and read through the last entry in the Z volume and then began again. This gave him a broad overview of many things and introduced him to subjects he wanted to learn more about.

No one with access to a local library or the Internet should ever stop learning. Throughout most of recorded history, people made a living based on what they could do. But here in the information age, we make a living and create success based on what we know.

We should look upon learning much like we view making a deposit in the bank. When we put money in our account, our balance grows, and when we learn something, our knowledge and wisdom balance can be increased.

The most famous person from my home state of Oklahoma and arguably the most famous individual of his era was Will Rogers. I featured Will Rogers in one of my *Homecoming Historical* novels and movies. Among the countless quotable statements he left us, the most enduring is the one etched in stone at his memorial site: "I never met a man I didn't like." I believe the same thing is true of books and all other learning resources. There are no subjects that are not valuable to learn about. People at the top of any field of endeavor know more than everyone else about a specific topic.

Learning must become a habit. Whether you read books, access lectures, or watch documentaries, you must always be building your bank of knowledge via learning. This form of consistent learning will result in periodic quantum leaps I call enlightenment.

When I was in the fourth grade, our class was struggling through the tedious process of learning fractions.

Those in the field of formal education must realize that ignorance is not your enemy; instead, boredom is your enemy. There are no subjects or topics that cannot be made to be absolutely fascinating, but in the fourth grade I was struggling to learn fractions. Over many weeks, I was mystified by the entire concept. Then one afternoon without warning and for no particular reason I could discern, I got it. The accumulated information I had learned finally reached a critical mass, and I suddenly understood fractions.

Thomas Edison said, "We don't know a millionth of one percent about anything." This points out not only Edison's insatiable curiosity but his understanding of accumulating learning until critical mass is achieved.

I hope this book will not only teach you about the process of formal and informal learning but will propel you into the lifelong quest for knowledge, information, and wisdom. A person who has access to learning and remains ignorant is no better off than a hungry person presented with a banquet who starves to death.

CHAPTER TWO

THE PROCESS OF LEARNING: WHEN DOES LEARNING BEGIN?

RAY H. HULL, PHD

When does it begin? How does learning begin? One of the most difficult questions I have been attempting to answer is, "What *is* learning?" It seems like a simple question. Right? But, I have been asking my university colleagues that question, and their typical response has been one of silence, then a look of wonder, then more pondering, and then the usual answer, "That's a good question! I guess it is what we do throughout our life!"

That response has been a typical one from my learned university colleagues who have been professors for a number of years, teaching college-level students who are in their classes to *learn*.

So, what is learning? When does it begin? When does it end?

But, learning is simple. Right? It is the process of moving information from "out there"—from a textbook, from someone's mouth, from something we see—and making that knowledge ours. Sounds simple, but is it?

WHEN DOES LEARNING BEGIN?

Beginning in the 1920s, scientists such as the eminent Swiss psychologist Jean Piaget felt that the young human mind can be described in terms of complex cognitive structures (the process of thinking, remembering, reasoning, using language). From his close observations of infants and the questioning of children, he concluded that cognitive development proceeds through certain stages, each involving different cognitive schemes. He found that infants actually seek environmental stimulation that promotes their intellectual development; that their representations of objects, space, time, cause, and self are constructed gradually during the first 24 months after birth; and that the development of physical reality depends on the gradual coordination of looking, listening, and touching.[1]

WHEN DOES IT ACTUALLY BEGIN?

But, when does learning actually begin? Some authorities feel that learning begins before birth. It seems that the human auditory/hearing system is mature enough at about seven months after conception to hear the mother's voice and begin to be aware of both pleasant sounds coming from mother's voice and, on the other hand, angry/loud sounds from that same voice. When the sounds of her voice are pleasant and loving, electromyographic measurements of the movements of the unborn child show that the child tends to relax. If loud and angry sounds are emitted from mother, the muscles of the unborn child become tense, reflecting the emotional state of the mother.

How does this happen? How does the unborn child hear the sounds coming from mother's voice? Here is how. The unborn child's auditory system has, by seven months post-conception, developed into a functional mechanism for hearing. Further, the child is suspended in a fluid medium within the mother's uterus, which is one of the most efficient systems for the transmission of sound waves. As mother's voice is transmitted even more efficiently by way of her rib cage that vibrates as a result of her voice, those vibrations are sent very nicely into the embryonic fluid of the uterus where the unborn child is housed.

Even though the unborn child is hearing mother's voice loudly and clearly, the child is fairly well isolated from external sounds and his environment by the uterine wall, the bladder, and other tissues located outside of the uterus—the muscles of the abdominal wall, any fatty tissue that happens to be there, and the skin wall of the abdomen. In fact, some research indicates that the reduction of sound from the outside world is in the vicinity of 60 decibels. So, the unborn child is well isolated from the sounds outside of the mother. Therefore, the unborn child from about seven to nine months in a normal-term pregnancy is primarily listening to three sounds loudly and clearly—mother's voice and the emotions generated from it, the rushing sounds generated by the placenta, and an occasional belch or stomach growl from Mom.

They Learn Their Mother's Voice before Birth

So, even before birth, the child is at least receiving and in some ways responding to the sounds generated by the mother and the emotions emanating from her voice. In fact, research was conducted by measuring the action potential (nerve firing) generated by the muscles of the newborn infant in response to their mother's voice compared with the voices of women (usually nurses in the newborn nursery) who are not their mother.[2] The research was conducted using an electromyographer (EMG) that measures the action potential and movement of the muscles. A common phrase was used as the stimulus and was spoken approximately 16 inches above the baby's head. It was, "Hello (name of baby). I love you. You are a beautiful baby (name of baby), and your mother loves you sooooo much!" The mother was instructed to use what was considered to be a loving vocal melody when the phrase was uttered, with a great deal of gentle melodic up and down inflections in her voice. For this study, every newborn baby was surrounded by soft blankets and lying comfortably in a crib. The electrodes for the electromyographer were placed on the calf of one leg of the baby, away from movements of respiration, vocalizations, and heartbeat. Each baby was in a state of light sleep.

In each instance, when the baby's mother recited the phrase using the melodic inflections that were requested, the action potential of the baby's muscles reflected the inflections of their mother's voice in nearly an identical manner. In fact, the visualizations on the EMG screen nearly matched the inflections of the mother's voice. But, when a woman of nearly the same age (generally one of the nurses in the newborn nursery) used the same phrase and the same melodic intonation, the new born baby presented little or no response, or on occasion the response was a negative one. When the baby's mother was brought back to the baby's crib and gave the same phrase using the same melodic intonations that were previously instructed, the newborn baby's EMG responses once again reflected in a nearly identical manner the inflections of their mother's voice, indicating that the newborn baby recognized their mother's voice, but gave no response or a negative response to a strange woman's voice.

The baby had therefore apparently learned to recognize her or his mother's voice through exposure prior to being born. This author has always thought that that technique would be an excellent choice for a television mystery movie. If two women were demanding that the same baby was their own child and the story centered on that controversy, rather than engaging in DNA or other forms of complicated testing, let the baby tell them! That would solve the mystery!

Learning after Birth

After birth, of course babies continue to learn. They learn early on about the loving and comforting sounds coming from their mother when she enters the space where baby lies in the bassinette, and baby learns mother's scent as she gently picks up the baby and holds her or him in soft, warm blankets. Baby learns about and recognizes the loving sounds that come from mother's mouth, the sounds that the baby was taken away from at birth. Now they are back!

BABIES PUT TWO AND TWO TOGETHER

Baby learns other things early on in his or her life. The baby in the early months and even the early weeks after arriving home begins to put two and two together. For example, baby learns that the scents emanating from the kitchen mean that hunger will soon be relieved. The sounds of mother or father, the shuffling of feet, the rustling of clothing, or the door of their space opening means that they will be picked up and cradled in mom's or Dad's arms, and maybe their favorite "binkie" (pacifier) will sooth baby until next feeding.

As baby is putting two and two together—those things in the baby's life that mean soothing hunger or being cuddled and held and sung to—the baby begins putting other things into their repertoire of learning. They begin to recognize certain combinations of vocalized sounds that emanate from the mouths of their immediate family. The happy vocalized combinations of sounds are said over and over again: "Pretty baby!" "Love you," "Time to eat!" "Rock a bye baby in the tree tops…" "Cindy is such a pretty baby!" After "Cindy" is used over and over again and directed to the baby, the baby will begin to attach those combinations of sounds to herself and will eventually begin to recognize that name as belonging to her!

SO, IS BABY'S MIND A BLANK SLATE?

It was once commonly thought that an infant's mind was a blank slate, nor could a baby possess knowledge.

But, according to the National Academies of Science and other reliable sources,[3] it is known that very young children are competent, active agents of their own conceptual development. As stated earlier in this chapter, a major move away from the "blank slate" view of the infant mind was taken by Swiss psychologist Jean Piaget in the 1920s.

A wonderful summary of the enormous body of research that has come available over the past several decades relative to how children learn is provided by way of the National Academies of Science. For example, four major areas of research in this area are presented as follows:

An Early Predisposition to Learn

This describes an early predisposition to learn about some things but not others. It states that there is no evidence that infants come into the world as "blank slates." Rather, young children show positive biases to learn preferred types of information early in life. These forms of knowledge are referred to as "privileged domains"—broadly defined categories such as biological concepts, cause and effect, numbers, and language-based.[4]

Strategies and Metacognition

Child learners must depend on will, ingenuity, and effort to enhance their learning. It depends on the child and the child's intent on learning. The past 30 years have witnessed a great deal of research that reveals that children possess heretofore unrecognized strategic and metacognitive competence.[5]

Theories of Mind

This theory states that as children mature, they develop "theories" of what it means to learn and understand, which influence how they situate themselves in environments that require intentional learning.[6] According to a publication by the National Academies of Science,[7] not all learners come to school ready to learn in exactly the same way, and some authorities feel that there is more than one way to learn and more than one way to be "intelligent." Understanding that there are multiple intelligences may suggest ways of helping children learn by supporting their strengths and strengthening their weaknesses.

Children and Community

Even though a great deal of children's learning is self-motivated and self-directed, other people play major roles as guides in helping the development of learning in children. Not only do people serve as guides to learning, there are other tools such as television (in some moderation), books, videos, and other devices.[8]

SUGGESTIONS TO ENHANCE EARLY LEARNING

Learning requires children to pay attention, to observe, to memorize, to understand, and to some degree to take responsibility for their own learning. It is important that parents, early teachers, grandparents, and others who interact with children encourage and provide opportunities for children to explore, to build, to inquire, to seek out avenues for adventure, and to expand their "world model"—their vision of the world as they see it.

Here are some suggestions on how that can be:[9]

1. Avoid situations where children are passive listeners for long periods of time.

2. Provide children with hands-on activities, e.g. experiments, opportunities for hands-on observations, projects that involve them.

3. Encourage participation in discussions pertaining to activities and events that are of interest to them.

4. Take children (and other children—neighbors, cousins) to museums, the zoo, amusement parks that are more than merry go rounds, the airport to watch planes take off and land, a farm, the county or state fair, to plays and musical events, and on and on. There are so many that are available that can expand the child's "world model" and cause them to want to learn more.

5. Assist children in creating goals for learning that are consistent with their interests.

6. Provide children opportunities to take some control over their own learning. Taking control over one's learning means allowing children to make some decisions about the things they are learning about.

I remember growing up on our farm, and on a cool summer morning I might go into the shed where my father kept used lumber, tools, pieces of odds and ends that could be used to repair a feed trough, and other items that would catch my eye. I would take a few pieces of wood, a hammer, some nails, and some other scraps of materials and carry them to the back step of our farm house and "set up shop" on the concrete steps. From those pieces of wood and other materials, I would begin building. The design of what I was building would take shape in my mind, and then I would continue until the things I had imagined was complete. Those included a soap box derby car (wheels came later); an airplane; a tiny house with windows, doors, and a roof; and other things that I thought about, planned, and executed in my own time and my own way! In that way, I learned by doing, had fun, and in the meantime was satisfied with my accomplishments!

MAKE SURE THAT LEARNING EXPERIENCES ARE MEANINGFUL TO CHILDREN

Many activities that are designed entirely by parents or early educators are not meaningful to children because too often the children either do not understand why they are engaging in them or they do not recognize their purpose or their usefulness. Perhaps they are not culturally appropriate, or too frequently early educators in preschool, kindergarten, or first grade have activities that they have found in an activity publication that they think *every* child would enjoy. But for some of the children, the activity may have absolutely no meaning other than "doing something" to pass the time.

Parents and early educators can make learning activities more meaningful by using ones that have a more authentic context. For example, children can work on writing skills by allowing them to create a story (a creative writing project) rather than forcing them to engage in "writing practice" and learning the acceptable grammatical format of writing (which I personally found particularly boring!).

They can improve their communication skills by each giving a talk about a favorite pet, their summer vacation, or what they want to be when they grow up. Or, they can debate a topic on a pro and con basis. Even young children enjoy that activity.

Children can learn about science by engaging in an environment project or touring a medical laboratory.

However, in all ideas for learning, parents and early educators must keep cultural differences among children in mind.

ADJUSTING TO A NEW LEARNING ENVIRONMENT IN CHILDHOOD

I cannot help but recall my early experiences in learning that I gained while in the rural school I attended through the eighth grade. When I first began my education in that very small two-room school, I had just been transferred from an elementary school in town. The school that I attended in town was a cultural shock as compared to my quiet life on the farm where I had lived since birth. Playground fights were rather routine. As a child with a severe stuttering problem, I was picked on regularly, laughed at, and being called names was a regular occurrence. I was miserable. Plus, my teacher was merciless. She seemed to enjoy making children feel inadequate.

When I was taken from that environment and enrolled in the new, small, two-room rural school that my father had helped to found, the environment was quite different. Most of the other students were from a very conservative Mennonite community where my family also farmed and were kind, gentle, and warm in their response to me, a child who was from a family "of the world," as they called it, because we were not of the Mennonite faith and heritage but were of a different religious faith.

The school had two classrooms. One was the "upper class room," which meant it was for students in the fifth, sixth, seventh, and eighth grades. The "lower class room" contained first through fourth grade. Each room had their own teacher—one teacher for four grades in each of the two classrooms. Each row of students was a "class." So in the upper room, there were four rows of students, one for each grade. There were three of us in the fourth grade—two girls and myself. The environment was so different from that which I had become accustomed to in "town school" that it took me a while to learn about the new environment and *learn how to learn* in that new school.

As students advanced through the grades, the only thing that identified one's advancement was that one's current grade was moved into a row that was one row closer to the windows on the north side of the room nearest the highway.

As I said earlier, each year my grade had three students—two girls and me. In spite of the fact that I was considered a severe stutterer, I wasn't teased by the others. Most of the children were of a conservative Mennonite order, so their schooling ended at the eighth grade before graduating and going on with their life. They were gentle and nurturing children who I liked very much. The girls wore long print dresses, dark hose, plain shoes, and their hair was tightly braided under their white caps that had long straps that hung loosely around their shoulders. The boys wore blue jeans or rather loose, obviously homemade pants held into place with suspenders, high top shoes, high buttoned shirts, and a standard flat-crowned hat—either brown or black.

Because one teacher taught four different grades in each of the two classrooms, during four years we got to know her pretty well. And, because the lowest grades in each classroom heard all of the lessons of the higher grades each day, by the time one reached the upper grades of your room, you had experienced all of their lessons for two or three consecutive years, so you knew them nearly by heart by the time it was your turn!

WHAT I LEARNED FROM MY TEACHER, MRS. HAMILTON

My second year in that rural school found me in the fifth grade in the "upper class room." I had completed fourth grade in the "lower class room" and was graduated into the upper class room. That move transformed my life. Her name was Mrs. Hamilton. She was the teacher from whom I learned the most in those formative years and who I remember most fondly. I never did know her first name. I just knew her as Mrs. Hamilton. She wasn't beautiful, but she was pretty in a pleasant sort of way, and I thought she was absolutely wonderful! Through her, we learned beyond the academic subjects that were required of her to teach, and her influence has remained with me through these many years. Of all the many things I learned from her, I remember these to this day:

1. We learned academic honesty and integrity.

2. We learned about table etiquette when we began having hot lunches in the basement of our two-room school:

   a. Where the silverware was to be placed on the table;

   b. To seat the young lady next to you;

   c. Appropriate dinner conversation;

   d. To always be polite, and to ask that food be passed rather than reaching for it.

3. One day she brought sea shells from Hawaii that she had picked from the beach on a vacation. Most of us had never seen such pretty shells before, nor from our rather isolated vantage point in the middle of rural Kansas had we even thought about Hawaii except through our World Geography book. Hawaii seemed like a distant place to be seen only through pictures.

4. She brought fruits and vegetables that many of us had never seen nor tasted including pomegranate, papaya, mango, bok choy, and others. We all had the opportunity to taste them. We had never experienced such exotic tastes before, but we learned something new during those experiences with Mrs. Hamilton.

5. We learned about strict discipline in the classroom—that is, no whispering, no squirming, no turning around to look at the person behind you. However, no matter how strict the discipline, we learned that it could be administered with love and compassion.

6. We learned each day that she loved every one of us, no matter how smelly we were from doing farm chores before coming to school, wearing our smelly shoes, and usually only bathing once per week. By Friday, I imagine that many of us were fairly ripe!

7. We learned from her how to play fairly on the playground, which was simply an open field behind our school.

We continued to learn from Mrs. Hamilton even at the lunch table. At lunch time, when we began to have hot lunches at school, all of us sat around one long table in the basement of our school. With Mrs. Hamilton seated at the head of the table, she would have us all bow our heads in prayer as she led us in a prayer of thanks before we ate. Our school had received many sacks of government surplus white beans, so we ate white beans, mashed potatoes with white gravy, and corn bread quite frequently during one full year. In spite of the regularity of white beans and corn bread, the prayer of thanks was said each day. Our cooks were ladies with their long cotton print dresses, dark hose, plain shoes, and their hair pulled tightly under their black or dark blue Holdeman Mennonite caps. The white gravy that they made was from just flour and milk, and it tasted awful. However, we learned not to tell the cooks. Rather, we learned to thank them pleasantly for their work on our behalf.

On certain days when we were to bring our own sack lunches or a lunch pail because there would be no hot lunch downstairs, we ate quietly at our desks in our classroom. Mrs. Hamilton would sit at her desk while nibbling at her own lunch and would read us stories written by Laura Ingles Wilder, the *Little House on the Prairie* stories. We learned many things from those stories. We learned about the life of a family living on the prairie, about survival in terrible snow storms, about Native Americans, and other things. Those times were special to all of us. When she read, she read in such a way that it almost seemed that we were there with the Wilder family in that long winter! And, rather than simply ending each story, we continued learning as we discussed what we had heard and learned from what she had read to us.

Mrs. Hamilton is the one teacher I have remembered throughout the years. The others I have forgotten, except for the bad ones. I think about her from time to time, and I am sure that she has passed on by now. She was strict, but we knew that she loved us all. We were safe, nurtured, and would not only learn our subjects well but learned many other valuable lessons through her.

Rather than trying to find fault, we were praised for the good work that we accomplished. To me, it was a breath of fresh air that encouraged me to learn and to enjoy the process of learning each day.

THIS IS HOW CHILDREN LEARN

Research has repeatedly shown that children learn in many different ways. As children develop, they form new ways of representing their world. Each child develops their own "world model," which is their own personal concept of their personal world.

My world was very different from that of my acquaintances who lived in town or in the city. My world centered on open spaces in the country, including my "hiding place" out in the grove of trees about 100 yards north of our farmhouse next to the pasture where our dairy cows grazed and lounged each day. The hayloft above our large wooden barn was where I would play in the hay, and where I could think about life and make up games to play. My world model included getting my calf ready to show at the 4H fair in the summer, grieving over a dead cow, watching a baby calf being born, and then observing him or her searching for nourishment from the mother immediately after. Then, as I grew in age and strength, I was given responsibilities that involved work around the farm.

The "world model" of my acquaintances who lived in town seemed to be quite different—more confined to small yards, play that was inside their house, riding their bicycle on smooth streets and sidewalks rather than on rough gravel and sand roads like I had to try to negotiate, playing with friends who lived nearby, getting into fights over issues that seemed to be major ones in their eyes, going to the drug store for a soda, and others that to my way of thinking were from a different world, not mine.

LEARNING IS ACCOMPLISHED IN DIFFERENT WAYS

In the end, we realize that learning is accomplished in different ways by different children. The ingredients for learning include an open environment for learning, multiple opportunities for learning, rewards for learning, and recognition of accomplishments. On the other hand, however, there doesn't always have to be reward attached to learning because there should also be an intrinsic motivation for learning. For example, the child who likes to put puzzles together for the fun of it. The child who enjoys building a soap box derby car for the purpose of entering a race. If she or he wins, then the reward comes from the accomplishment of winning or, if not winning, at least participating and finishing the race!

ENCOURAGING CHILDREN TO LEARN

When we are encouraging children to learn, there are some things to remember:

- We should recognize their accomplishments and not chastise for failure.

- Recognize children's accomplishments by internal factors (recognizing their great imagination, their ideas, their hard work) rather than external ones (the result of a positive work environment, or they succeeded because of the help they received from others).

- Encourage children to believe in themselves.

- Provide feedback, not with criticism but to give constructive instruction.

- Help children set realistic goals, not to restrict (you probably won't be able to do all of that!) but goals that should be able to be accomplished, and the child is encouraged to complete them.

- Encourage novel or interesting tasks that challenge them but are kept at a realistic level that should be able to be accomplished.

That is how learning occurs. That is how learning becomes real.

NOTES

1. National Research Council, *How People Learn: Brain, Mind, Experience, and School: Expanded Edition* (Washington, DC: The National Academies Press, 2000), https://www.nap.edu/9853/.

2. R. Hull, "Electromyographic Responses of Newborns to Mother's Voice," (Unpublished research, University of Northern Colorado, 1990).

3. S. Carey and R. Gelman, The Epigenesist of the Mind: Essays on Biology and Cognition (Hillsdale, NJ: Lawrence Erlbaum Publishers, 1991); H. Gardner, The Unschooled Mind: How Children Think and How Schools Should Teach (New York: Basic Books, 1991); Jean Piaget, Success and Understanding (Cambridge, MA: Harvard University Press, 1978).

4. Carey and Gelman, The Epigenesist of the Mind.

5. J. Brown, A. Collins, and P. Duguid, "Situated Cognition and the Culture of Learning," *Educational Researcher* (Washington, D.C, 1989) 18; J. DeLoache, et. al., *American Psychological Society* 9, (1998), 205-210.

6. C. Berieter, "Situated Cognition and How to Overcome It," qtd. in D. Kirshner and J. Whitson, eds., *Situated Cognition: Social, Semiotic, and Psychological Perspectives*, (Hillsdale, NJ: Lawrence Erlbaum Publishers), 281-300.

7. National Research Council, *How People Learn*.

8. J. Wright and A. Huston, "The Relationship of Early Television Viewing to School Readiness and Vocabulary of Children from Low Income Families: The Early Window Project," *Child Development* 71, (2001), 1347-1366.

9. R. Elmore, P. Peterson, and S. McCarthy, *Restructuring in the Classroom: Teaching, Learning and School Organization*, (San Francisco, CA: Jossey-Bass Publishing, 1996); M. Scardamalia and C. Berieter, "Higher Levels of Agency for Children in Knowledge Building: A Challenge for the Design of New Knowledge Media," *Learning Sciences* 1, (1991), 37-68; Piaget, *Success and Understanding.*

CHAPTER THREE

LEARNING TO LEARN

JIM STOVALL

Learning is among the most normal and natural functions of any human being. We are learning virtually from our birth, and the first few years of life represent one of our most prolific periods of learning. We naturally learn in a very fluid, unobtrusive way, and ironically some of our best learning occurs when we don't even realize it's happening.

My first employee and colleague in my company, the Narrative Television Network, was diagnosed with terminal cancer many years ago. As a single mother, she decided to make me the guardian of her teenaged daughter. That daughter has grown up to be a very impressive and formidable young woman now raising a child of her own.

At this writing, her son is two and a half years old and is a virtual learning machine. He has learned to speak English, Spanish, and American Sign Language. Grown adults trying to learn English as a second language will tell you that it is one of the most difficult languages to learn and master, but this two-and-a-half-year-old child can go from English to Spanish to sign language and back again effortlessly within one brief conversation. The most amazing and pertinent thing about it is that he is unaware that he has learned anything.

In a thought-provoking sort of way, formal education alters and in some ways can disrupt our natural learning process. We naturally learn as a result of our innate curiosity about everything and everyone around us. This is when human beings learn best.

If you've ever been around a small child for any length of time, you are well aware that they ask a myriad of questions. Invariably, each of your answers invokes another one of their questions. Oftentimes, the response to each of your explanations is a simple "Why?"

As we pursue our formal education in school and our career training on the job, we are no longer encouraged or in some cases even allowed to ask questions that are not strictly within some narrowly defined guidelines.

Our best learning occurs when it is fun, interesting, and free-flowing. Unfortunately, our formal education and career training somehow succeeds in making everything mundane and boring.

My first novel, *The Ultimate Gift*, was turned into a major motion picture from 20th Century Fox starring James Garner, Abigail Breslin, and Brian Dennehy. That book and movie opened many doors in my life, which have resulted in many more films, books, and the opportunity to be a part of having *The Ultimate Gift's* message become part of the curriculum in hundreds of public and private schools across the country and around the world.

I get to visit a number of schools and meet the students and teachers in their classrooms. Several times each year, I do satellite sessions with many schools across the country all at the same time as we discuss the messages and lessons in *The Ultimate Gift* book and movie.

Observing the learning process within the classroom has been enlightening for me. I remember one particular day when I was visiting a middle school to speak to the kids at the end of their history class. I got there early and experienced hundreds of 12- to 15-year-old young people in the halls between classes. They were fully engaged, totally lively, and completely energized. These kids were carrying on multiple conversations as they observed everything and everyone around them. Then an amazing transformation took place as the bell rang and these same middle school students settled into their seats within their history class. It was almost like a light switch had been turned off. They became listless, dull, and unengaged.

The teacher told them where to sit, when to sit, and how to sit. Then after a few brief monotone announcements, the history teacher launched into a well-worn, over-prepared, boring lecture about World War II.

As I mentioned in a previous chapter, thanks to high-speed audiobooks I am a voracious reader, and among my favorite topics is the study of World War II and biographies of people who lived through that historic era.

As I sat listening to the history teacher mechanically drone on about what otherwise should be one of the most exciting and thought-provoking points in human history, I was struck by the fact that the film legend Tom Hanks had just spent millions of dollars of studio capital to create his epic film masterpiece about

World War II entitled *Saving Private Ryan*. That movie received both critical acclaim as well as becoming a runaway box office success.

I had just enjoyed that film for the second time a few nights before my challenging experience in the middle school history class. If World War II can be made boring, anything can. Those of us who want to teach, instruct, train, or educate must realize it is our responsibility to make our topic relevant, engaging, and compelling.

Although my portion of this book is mostly limited to the informal part of our learning and education, I'm a huge believer in the power and value of a formal education. I am very proud of my own university degree and have founded a scholarship that over the last 25 years has given financial support to over 500 college students.

As a professional speaker, I am often hired to give speeches to colleges and universities. While on campus, I often lecture in business, law, or media classes. Invariably, the professor will give me a cursory introduction and then turn the class over to me. Almost without fail on these occasions, one or more college students will ask questions such as, "Will this be on the test?"; "Is attendance required?"; "Should we take notes?"; or "Why does this matter?" This always gives me the opportunity to present these students with my perspective on education and learning.

First, I give them a few staggering statistics about the cost of a college education and remind them that someone in their life—be it a parent, grandparent, or other individual who loves them—made a major financial commitment so they could be in the classroom today. I further remind them that many gathered in the room are racking up untold thousands of dollars of student loan debt that will have to be paid off, with interest, at some point in their future.

I ask them to recall the time when they were in high school and excitedly filled out college applications including one to this institution where I am speaking in their class. It never ceases to amaze me that all the time, effort, and energy that went into applying for and getting into college is followed by an attitude that can best be summed up with "What's the least I can do and get out of here?"

It seems to me that many in our world today want the benefits of a higher education without really desiring to learn anything at all. If you're going to go to the time and expense of attending a university or any other learning institution, why wouldn't you want to get everything out of it you could?

You don't pay for overpriced Broadway tickets and then arrive late, ignore the show, and leave early. You don't go to an expensive restaurant, meticulously review the menu, and order your favorite meal only to brush it aside and walk away. Why do we treat education like something we desire until we get involved and then treat it like something we must endure?

Learning should be fun, fascinating, and compelling. The best learning occurs when the learner is unaware it even happened. People who watched *Saving Private Ryan* probably learned more about World War II than the middle school students who studied that conflict for an entire semester.

There are no boring subjects. There are boring teachers, presentations, and lessons. If you're going to teach anyone anything, questions like "Why does this matter?" deserve well thought out and quality answers.

If you read any of my books, watch my movies, review my weekly syndicated columns, or attend my speeches, you will know within a few moments what I think is important and why it matters to you.

Education is a presentation while learning is a process. It is a give-and-take proposition. You've heard it said that when the pupil is ready, the teacher will arrive. I can assure you the pupil will be ready when he or she understands why this matters and what role it will play in their lives.

When I was attending college, I had the privilege of learning from an enlightened educator named Dr. Harold Paul. Prior to entering that university, I had been a poor, unengaged student, and my grades had been mediocre at best. I had always relied upon my athletic prowess thinking it would get me through school and everything else in life. Then after being diagnosed with a condition that would result in my blindness, I realized my football career was over, and I wasn't even going to be able to read written words on a page or chalkboard much longer.

Dr. Paul taught humanities, and I remember being in the midst of an intense study of Dante's *Inferno*. To say the least, I didn't understand it or relate to it, but Dr. Paul's enthusiasm for the subject held my attention until I could begin to glimpse the majesty and power of Dante's work.

At the end of the semester, I thanked Dr. Paul and told him I appreciated Dante but didn't fully understand his writing. Dr. Paul assured me, "Dante will be there throughout your life whenever you are ready." This has proven to be valid in my life many times.

Most of us have had the experience of reading scriptures or other significant writings that are reread often. Invariably, we read a passage that we know we have read countless times before but somehow discover something that had never been apparent to us in previous readings.

Whether it's a person you get to know better, a place you visit often, or a book you reread, there is always more to learn and experience.

Sir Edmund Hillary will always be remembered as the first person to climb Mount Everest. While his successful ascent to the top of the world is inspiring, we can find some additional inspiration in his previous failed attempts to climb the great mountain and an often-repeated anecdote about him.

After having to turn back on several attempts to reach the summit, Hillary funded his subsequent expeditions by giving lectures. In all his lectures, he stood on a stage in front of a huge photo of Mount Everest. After talking to his audience for over an hour, he would end each of his speeches by assuring the crowd, "Our best attempts to climb to the top of the world have all failed to date." Then Hillary would turn toward the giant photo behind him and speak directly to the mountain as he concluded his speech saying, "But we will inevitably succeed because you can't get any bigger, and I can."

This type of thinking should be applied to all of our learning and training. Things we are not able to master or fully master today may be readily understandable and applicable in the future.

Our learning must always be celebrated with the introduction of more things to be learned. Just as the mountain climber only sees the incline in front of him until he reaches the summit when the whole world opens up, achieving one pinnacle in learning reveals more mountains to climb and information to master.

The great challenges, diseases, and problems in our world can be overcome because, as Hillary reminds us, they can't get any bigger while we individually and collectively can. As we come to understand this, we inevitably realize that—like sleeping, eating, and breathing—learning can never stop. Learning is not a chore or duty to be endured or tolerated. It is a privilege and pleasure to be savored.

As a stockholder in Warren Buffett's company, I have participated in many conference calls and meetings with him. Among the most memorable statements I have heard Warren Buffett make is, "People know the cost of everything and the value of nothing." This is certainly true when it comes to education. While we all lament the cost of education, we often fail to calculate the value it brings to our lives and to the world. We cannot fully understand the price of learning until we acknowledge the cost of ignorance.

My late, great friend, colleague, and mentor Zig Ziglar told me late in his career that he had been giving incorrect information to his audiences and readers for years. He explained that while on stage he would strike a defiant pose and in a strained voice declare, "You've got to pay the price for success." As the elder statesman in the writing and speaking industry, Zig told me he had discovered, "We don't really pay the price for success. We enjoy the price of success and pay the price for failure."

The answer to virtually any question, problem, or challenge you will face in your personal or professional life is to learn more.

If success in business is calculated and defined by money, it is ironic that most people believe that if you took all the money in the world and divided it up equally among the entire population, in a few short months or years the rich would be rich again and the poor would be poor again. This illustrates that money is not the key to success or wealth. Knowledge is the key to success, wealth, and anything we want in our lives.

Information abounds in our world. Throughout most of recorded history, a book or even a few pages were valued more than gold or silver. Today, we have books that go unread and lectures that go unattended.

The most valued and utilized businesses in the world today feature search engines that help us to sift through all the voluminous information we have available to us. Once we have the information, we must, however, not fail to use it. A lesson learned but not applied is a waste of time and money.

We live in a world where, when it's all said and done, there's a lot said and very little done. While I think it's vital we all continue to learn throughout our lives, most of us already know more than is necessary to succeed at a higher level and reach most of our goals. We don't fail because we don't know what to do. We fail because we don't do what we know.

If information alone was success, we would all be rich, thin, and happy. Commit that you will not be among those ignorant souls who had access to learning but didn't take advantage of it or those unproductive, selfish souls who learned lessons that were never applied.

Learning is nothing more than curiosity, awareness, and persistence. Success comes when we use that which we have learned in the service of others.

CHAPTER FOUR

THE NEUROSCIENCE OF LEARNING

RAY H. HULL, PHD

The human brain is a fantastically complicated computer, more complex than any that have been developed up to the present time. Its complexity is mind boggling! For example, the human brain is made up of approximately 100,000,000,000 (100 billion) neurons (storage and processing nerve cells), interacting with each other by way of approximately 1,000,000,000,000,000 (1 quadrillion) transmitting connectors (synapses).[1]

> A neuron is an electrically excitable cell that processes and transmits information by electro-chemical signaling [sic]. ...Each neuron may be connected to up to 10,000 other neurons, passing signals to each other via as many as 1,000 trillion synaptic connections, equivalent by some estimates to a computer with a 1 trillion bit per second processor. Estimates of the human brain's memory capacity vary widely from 1 to 1,000 terabytes (for comparison, the 19 million volumes in the US Library of Congress represents about 10 terabytes of data).[2]

The brain is supported by another approximately 1 quadrillion glial cells (neuroglia) called astrocytes, oligodendrocytes, and microglia, which are microscopic cells with fibrils, or sub-microscopic fibers, that reach out and attach themselves to nerve cells throughout the brain. They function to provide nutrient support, physical support, repair of the nerve cells (neurons), and also allow for communication to take place between neurons so that the central nervous system can continue to function smoothly. These glial cells also assist with the neuroplasticity of the brain, or the ability of the brain to transfer duties between its various functional parts as a result of injury or insult, or to adjust or change function between areas of the brain as needed.

The human brain is never quiet. It is continually changing, developing new nerve cells, new neuronal connectors, new terminals that can transmit data into memory banks. It is ever changing and expanding.

AMAZING, ISN'T IT?

If the above isn't amazing enough, here's more! Information transmission within the human brain that takes place during the process of memory (information processing and retrieval) is achieved using electrochemical energy. Every neuron maintains an electrical voltage gradient across its cell membrane (covering), which is the result of differences in the ions of sodium, potassium, chloride, and calcium within the neuron (nerve cell). If the voltage changes significantly, an electrochemical spike called an action potential (or nerve impulse) is generated.

The nerve impulse travels in mini-microseconds along the nerve cell's axon (transmitter) and is transferred across a specialized connection (a synapse) onto a neighboring nerve cell, which receives the signal by way of its feathery dendritic connections (complex, wire-like receivers with multiple connectors). The synapse is a complex receiving/transmitting system with a gap between it and the connector from the neighboring cell, across which the electrical signal crosses to the next nerve cell. The gap, called a synaptic cleft is approximately 20 nanometers across, or 20 millionths of a millimeter. A typical nerve cell fires at a rate of 5 to 50 times every second.

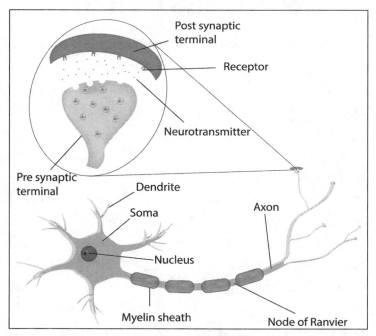

Figure 1: Illustration of nerve fibers with associated synaptic connections.

To make this complex human computer even more complicated, each individual neuron (nerve cell) can form thousands of links with other neurons, giving the typical brain well over 1,000 trillion synaptic connectors. Interestingly, unlike a commercial computer, the connections between neurons are not static. They can change over time. The more signals sent between two neurons, the stronger the connection grows, and so with each new experience or each remembered event in our lives or each new fact or word learned, the brain slightly rewires itself in order to store that information.

THE NEUROSCIENCE OF LEARNING

Now that we have completed our brief lesson in neuroscience, let's talk about how the brain works to allow us to learn throughout our lives. Figure 2 (below) gives us a picture of the various areas of the brain, or at least a glimpse of what each large area (or lobe) is responsible for in regard to everyday functioning, including learning and utilizing new information. For purposes of reference, the *pink shaded areas* include the frontal lobe and the temporal lobes. The *red and dark blue areas* in the middle of the brain include the motor strip, which controls movements from blinking our eyes (at the bottom) to wiggling our toes (at the top). The *light blue areas* include (at the top) the parietal lobe (pain, touch, and temperature), and (light blue in the back of the brain) the areas that control visual perception (visual recognition).

To simplify things by way of a very nice description by Edelson,[3] the brain can be thought of as a small football sitting on top of a stick, with the brain, per se, being the ball. The outer portion of the ball surrounds part of the middle of the brain known as the basal ganglia, which controls motor tone and involuntary motor activity. The basal ganglia also has a role in learning and in emotional regulation. The stick below the ball is known as the brain stem. The brain stem works to regulate body functions automatically, including some of the workings of the heart and blood supply system and including wakefulness and sleep, pre-analysis of hearing, vision, pain, touch, temperature, and most other information that is pre-processed before it reaches the brain, where it is then analyzed and used.

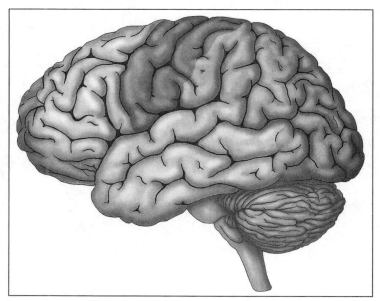

Figure 2: The lobes of the brain.

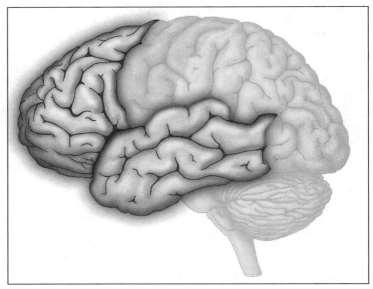

Figure 2a: The frontal and temporal lobe.

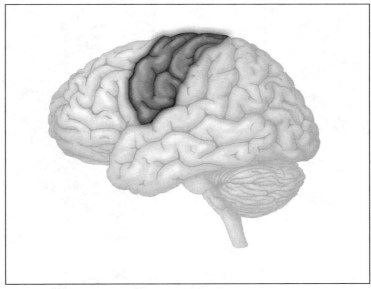

Figure 2b: The eye movement, motor, and speech section of the brain.

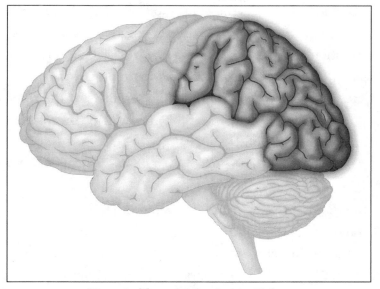

Figure 2c: The occiptal and parietal lobes.

The cortex, or outer layer of the football (the brain), is divided into two specialized halves. In most individuals who are right-handed, the left half of the brain controls language and is generally referred to as the dominant hemisphere. Specifically, this involves speaking and understanding words, remembering them, reading and spelling, and reasoning with them. The right half of the brain involves visual spatial abilities, often thought of as helping our hands do what our eyes see. It is called the non-dominant hemisphere. These skills entail understanding spatial relationships, recognizing how objects can be put together or taken apart, and remembering information that is seen.

The *frontal lobes* make up the front half of the brain and affect reasoning, judgment, emotional regulation, attention, planning, and organization. The posterior part (back portion that contains the motor strip) of the left frontal lobe controls the motor abilities of the right side of the body, and the right motor strip controls the left side of the body.

The left and right *parietal lobes*, generally above the ears and toward the upper part of the brain in back of the motor strip, mediate utilization of language, understanding spatial concepts, and also interpretation of the sensations of pain, touch, and temperature. The anterior (frontal) part of the left parietal lobe regulates appreciation of sensation (pain, touch, and temperature) for the right half of the body, and the anterior right parietal lobe does the same for the left side of the body.

The *temporal lobes*, located below the other parts of the brain and almost in line with the ears, involve hearing as well as auditory memory. The left temporal lobe also mediates memory of words and storage of language, and the right temporal lobe visual memory and storage of language.

The *occipital lobe*, in the back of the brain, controls vision and visual perception/recognition. Below the occipital lobe is the cerebellum, which regulates balance, and both coordinate movement and thinking.

LET'S LOOK A LITTLE FURTHER INTO THIS SOPHISTICATED COMPUTER SYSTEM

We'll begin at the back (posterior) part of the brain and work our way forward.

The Occipital Lobe

The occipital lobe is not only important because it allows us to see (see Figure 2c) but to also understand what our eyes are seeing. If the occipital pole (that tiny dark blue area referred to above) were damaged or destroyed, even if the eyes were perfectly normal we would not be able to see or perhaps process what we saw because that tiny area is what receives visual information from our eyes by way of the brain stem. Going a little deeper into the occipital lobe, that area allows us to learn about what we see. For example, we can learn that a specific image of a structure represents a house, or a specific shape of a furry animal is a dog, and so on. Even deeper in the occipital lobe we learn that, for example, that is *my* house, that is Scruffy *my* dog. We can see from combinations of printed images on a page that they are *words* that have meaning to us, both script and printed if we have learned to decipher those symbols. Also, when we are writing a letter or writing on a blackboard, that area of the brain allows us to recognize what we have written. If that area is damaged, we may be able to write, but in looking at what we wrote, we may not be able to understand what it says.

The *occipital lobe* also has inner connections with the *temporal lobe* that store and process auditory/verbal information. For example, when we hear the specific frequency and quality of voice, we can recognize it as the voice that is similar to that of our mother or father, and we visualize mother or father in our mind. When we hear a dog bark that sounds like our dog, we will unconsciously visualize our dog, even though we realize that what we heard could not be our dog because our dog is at home.

Those all seem to be simple visual tasks, but it takes a very complicated, or should I say highly sophisticated, central nervous system to engage in those mental gymnastics!

The Temporal Lobe

In observing Figure 2a further, the temporal lobe is located in the large shaded area on the lower side of the brain. This large lobe of the brain mainly processes what we hear, including the sounds of our environment, what people are saying, music (although music involves a number of areas of the brain for processing), and other things that we hear. This lobe is also important because it is critical to our ability to comprehend and understand speech. Everything that is heard by our ears is sent to the temporal lobe for processing. The temporal lobe is also responsible for storing and processing our verbal vocabulary, the words that we learn from babyhood into adulthood, their meaningful sequencing into sentences and thoughts, and the learning of new vocabulary words throughout our life.

The temporal lobe is associated rather closely to the occipital lobe for vision and allows us to process sensory input into meaningful information for processing and retention of visual memory, language comprehension, and association of emotions that pertain to what we hear and see.

Memory—whether short-term, intermediate-term, or long-term memory—is in some ways processed by way of the temporal lobe and its associations with the occipital lobe and, further on into the brain, the hippocampus. The hippocampus is critical for memory formation and retention (see Figure 3 for an illustration and the location of the hippocampus).

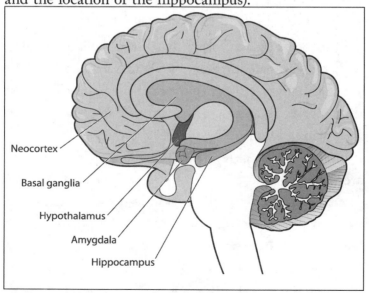

Neocortex

Basal ganglia

Hypothalamus

Amygdala

Hippocampus

Figure 3: Illustration and location of the hippocampus of the human brain.

The Parietal Lobe[4]

The parietal lobe, shown in the lighter shaded area on the upper portion of the brain in Figure 2c, is found above and to the left of the occipital lobe. The parietal lobe integrates sensory information, sensing the various parts of our bodies (feeling indigestion, sore muscles, sensing the position of our tongue inside of our mouth, and so on)—and including our sense of touch.

The parietal lobe also processes information regarding our sensations of touch, pain, and temperature from all parts of our body. We are able to sense pressure, for example when someone touches us, or pushes against us. If we get up in the middle of the night and stub our toe, we know instinctively that in about two milliseconds we are going to experience pain, and the pain might be slight or severe!

Further, it is interesting that the parietal lobes allow us to discriminate information via touch alone. If a person is visually impaired, this area of the brain along with the pressure receptors in the tips of one's fingers allow for learning braille. We can feel the difference between a dime and a quarter without seeing them when we are trying to find the right one in our pocket. We can discriminate writing on our skin by touch alone, or we know where a person is touching us by identifying its location by the sensation.

In relation to the above, one of my patients, a 14 year old female who became both profoundly hearing impaired and visually impaired learned to communicate by having the person "talking" to her write in the palm of her hand. The amazing aspect of this was that she wanted those who communicated with her to use cursive rather than print when writing in the palm of her hand. I could write, using cursive, as fast as I could talk, and she could still understand everything I was writing. She was so good at communicating in that manner that many of us thought that perhaps her deafness and blindness was psychogenic in nature. But, it was found that, indeed, she was both deaf and blind as a result of sudden onset.

The Frontal Lobe[5]

The frontal lobe is identified as the large shaded area area in Figure 2a located in the front and toward the middle of the brain. It is thought that the two hemispheres that divide the frontal lobe have different, but somewhat related functions. They are generally described in terms of the right hemisphere as the portion that allows us to think creatively, and the left that helps us to think logically.

A pre-frontal lobe is located posteriorly (toward the middle of the frontal lobe—not shaded). That area does not appear to mature until a person has reached their early to middle twenties. This area of the brain an provides us the ability to make rational and appropriate decisions about actions that we may be considering. In the immature brain (teenage years, for example), those decisions include engaging in unintelligent activities such as reckless driving, driving while intoxicated, taking chances that may cause an unpleasant result, and the many others that teenagers and very young adults may engage in. As that area matures, more rational decisions about our lives can evolve, or at least we hope so.

The pre-frontal lobes also possess the ability to access information and memories that we accumulate through learning that, for example, remind us how to communicate and interact appropriately in social or public situations. This area is responsible for our ability to show empathy or feel sorrow, and it allows us to understand the thinking and experiences of others and appreciate them. This understanding helps us to take cues as to how to behave or respond in various situations, including such situations as job interviews, and to understand the punch line of a joke. Our personality lives in our frontal lobes where emotions, problem-solving, reasoning, planning, decision-making, and information that we are learn throughout our lives are processed and used.

Motor Cortex of the Brain

The section of the brain numbered 2b is frequently called the motor strip of the brain because of what it does. It functions to control, from bottom to top, the movements of the lips, tongue, vocal mechanism, and then further up, the arms, shoulders, and further up, the legs, feet, toes, and so on. If an area of the motor strip is injured or does not mature, that area of the body may be impaired in regard to its functioning. The cerebellum and basal ganglia also assist this area of the brain by working to allow for smoothness and control of muscular movement.

ONE MORE THOUGHT

The human brain, as stated earlier, is an amazing computer. One has not been designed that can compare in regard to complexity, flexibility, or the ability to expand and change as new information is gained through it without being reprogrammed. The neuroscience of learning is forever changing as we go through our lives increasing our vocabulary, learning new avenues for efficiency in our jobs, meeting new people and developing our opinions regarding our willingness or desire to get to know them better, getting over disappointments, achieving new opportunities in and out of our personal and occupational lives.

We are continually learning, changing, seeking new information, achieving new goals, inventing new ideas, learning to play a new instrument, reading a new book, preparing a presentation for our next meeting. We continually seek change, learn about the care and feeding of our new four legged family member, and look for new frontiers of challenge.

Those all involve *learning*, retaining old information, and gathering new ideas and avenues for learning.

When those occur, we generally do not even think about the trillions of central nervous system events that are occurring within our brain each microsecond of our lives. The human brain is, indeed, an amazing piece of computing equipment. But it goes beyond that simple analogy. It is a God-given gift of amazing complexity that humans have yet to duplicate and probably never will. It is too flexible, too complex, too able to make subtle adjustments within itself, and too able to transfer important functions if one area becomes impaired.

It is, in the end, what makes us human.

NOTES

1. Mario Garrett, "Complexity of Our Brain," Psychology Today, February 25, 2014, https://www.psychologytoday.com/blog/iage/201402/complexity-our-brain.

2. Luke Mastin, "Neurons & Synapses," The Human Memory, accessed June 30, 2017, http://www.human-memory.net/brain_neurons.html.

3. R. Edelson, "The Dementias and Their Impact on Communication," qtd. in R. Hull, ed., *Communication Disorders in Aging*, (San Diego, CA: Plural Publishers, 2017).

4. Wikipedia, "Parietal lobe," June 28, 2017, https://en.wikipedia.org/wiki/Parietal_lobe.

5. Wikipedia, "Frontal lobe," June 28, 2017, https://en.wikipedia.org/wiki/Frontal_lobe.

CHAPTER FIVE

LEARNING TO LIVE

JIM STOVALL

I remember hearing a radio commercial for an adult education technical career school. In the commercial, an announcer excitedly repeated, "Learn so you can earn." While this chapter will focus on how learning plays a critical role in our business life and career, there are many rewards for learning beyond money.

I met one of my earliest mentors, Lee Braxton, when I was in college. Mr. Braxton had a sixth grade education and dropped out of school to earn a living for his family during the Great Depression. As a young entrepreneur, he earned millions of dollars, gave most of it away to charities, and volunteered for a nonprofit organization for the rest of his life as he simply lived off of his investments.

While I was in school, I asked him which degree program would be the best if I wanted to go into business for myself. Thinking he would tell me to get a degree in management, business law, or accounting, I was shocked when he said, "Learn about people. Money is constant and never changes, but people will be critical to your success."

I completed my university degree in psychology and sociology, and then—knowing no one would hire a young, blind, former football player—I told Mr. Braxton I wanted to become an entrepreneur. His advice was to read *Think and Grow Rich* by Napoleon Hill several times and come back to see him. That book and the teachings of Napoleon Hill became the basis for Mr. Braxton's mentorship and much of my success in business.

I believe we should never take advice from anybody who doesn't have what we want. Whether it's bankrupt financial advisors, overweight diet doctors, or morally corrupt religious leaders, it's not only important what people say but what they do.

If you were to poll successful entrepreneurs, self-made millionaires, and Fortune 500 executives to inquire about the most influential book in their career, more of them would name *Think and Grow Rich* by Napoleon Hill than any other book. I was very pleased to be able to chronicle highlights of Napoleon Hill's life in my novel *Top of the Hill*. A movie of that story is in the works, and it's exciting to bring Napoleon Hill, who was born in the 19th century and changed the world in the 20th century, into the 21st century.

Napoleon Hill was born in the 1880s in an impoverished part of rural Virginia. As a young newspaper reporter, he got an interview with Andrew Carnegie, the founder of US Steel. Young Napoleon Hill asked Carnegie about the secret of success and becoming rich. Andrew Carnegie explained that no one had ever fully explored and quantified the science of success, but if Napoleon Hill would commit 20 years of his life to the project, Carnegie would open the doors. Hill agreed, and Mr. Carnegie arranged for him to interview 500 successful leaders of the day including Thomas Edison, Henry Ford, Alexander Graham Bell, and many others.

Napoleon Hill's interviews became the basis for his groundbreaking book *Think and Grow Rich* that was released in 1937. Many people mistakenly believe that if you're not learning something that is current, it's not worth anything. Some of the greatest wisdom for us to learn is in old or even ancient texts.

While knowledge is valuable, wisdom is priceless. If you have a lot of knowledge, you will probably end up working for someone who has a lot of wisdom.

After I achieved my own success and wealth, I wrote a book entitled *The Millionaire Map,* which chronicled my journey from poverty to prosperity. Because Mr. Braxton and Napoleon Hill were both mentioned in that book, Don Green who runs The Napoleon Hill Foundation called me and asked if I had known that my mentor Lee Braxton and Napoleon Hill were best friends. I had never known this and was shocked to learn that my mentor, Mr. Braxton, had given the eulogy at Napoleon Hill's funeral.

The connection between me, Mr. Braxton, and Napoleon Hill has been the basis for a number of my books and much of my own learning. It's like the connection between knowledge, wisdom, and success. One you learn, one you apply, and one you experience throughout your life.

As I stated in an earlier chapter, the key to having a great idea is to go through your daily routine, wait for a problem to arise, and ask yourself, "How could I have avoided that?" The answer to that question is a great idea. The only thing you have to do to turn your great idea into a great business is to ask yourself, "How can I help other people avoid that problem?" The answer to that question is a great business idea.

Great ideas and businesses come from problems, and in my case, a big problem gave birth to a big idea that became a big business.

I remember, as if it were yesterday, waking up that morning and suddenly realizing I had lost the remainder of my sight. I was 29 years old, I had never met a blind person, and I didn't have a clue what I was going to do with the rest of my life. The only plan I could come up with that fateful morning involved moving into a little 9- by 12-foot room in the back of my house where I gathered my radio, my telephone, and my tape recorder. This little space became my whole world, and I really fully intended to never leave that room again.

The thought of running a large business, writing over 40 books with seven of them being made into movies, speaking to millions of people in arena events, or creating a weekly syndicated column read by countless people throughout North America, Europe, and Asia seemed as foreign to me as going to the moon.

I sat in my little self-imposed prison in the back of my house day after day, getting more depressed and more discouraged.

Two opportunities to learn about my situation presented themselves to me in my little room. First, I got a visit from a government employee who worked with blind and visually impaired people. He told me I would never have a job, earn money, or have friends like everyone else, and I needed to learn how to use a white cane, read Braille, and give up on my dreams.

The second opportunity to learn that came into my life at that critical point was an audiotape from the great author and speaker Dr. Denis Waitley. Denis had been a Blue Angel pilot and had written psychological profiles of prisoners of war returning from Vietnam along with Olympic athletes from the U.S. team.

His research into both prisoners and champions became the basis for his influential book *The Psychology of Winning*. On that audiotape given to me by an elderly neighbor, Dr. Waitley recited his epic poem *If You Think You Can, You Can*. So as I sat in my little 9- by 12-foot room that made up my whole universe, on one side of my chair was a white cane and the message involving lowering my expectations and giving up on my dreams. On the other side of my chair was my tape recorder, which constantly repeated Dr. Waitley's message *If You Think You Can, You Can*.

I realized someone was lying to me, and I chose to believe Dr. Waitley.

At that moment, I discovered a powerful truth about the process of learning. We get to choose what we learn, when we learn, who we learn from, and how we apply it. Our minds are among the most powerful resources in the universe, but they are only as valuable as the information we learn and apply.

Dr. Waitley's message stayed with me, and he wrote the foreword to my very first book entitled *You Don't Have To Be Blind To See*. He has been a great mentor in my life and remains among my best friends to this day.

As I sat in my 9- by 12-foot room, I was still totally blind and dealing with all the fears and doubts, but I had learned something I had not known before. I had learned that "If you think you can, you can." While my sight was gone, learning that lesson gave me visions of hope and possibility.

Prior to losing my sight, the little 9- by 12-foot room in the back of my house had been our television room. In the corner across from me sat a television, a video player, and my collection of classic movies. I have always been a fan of John Wayne, Kathryn Hepburn, Jimmy Stewart, and the other great stars of that era.

One day out of sheer boredom I put on one of those old movies thinking that because I had seen it so many times, I would be able to just listen to the soundtrack and follow the story. It was a movie entitled *The Big Sleep* starring Humphrey Bogart.

As the video played, the soundtrack reminded me of the images on the screen that I could no longer see. Then I was overwhelmed when I heard a gunshot, a car speeding away, and dramatic music. I lost the thread of the plot, became extremely frustrated, and heard myself say what I know now to be the magic words: "Somebody ought to do something about that." The next time you get frustrated and hear yourself say those magic words, you just had a great idea and potentially a great business opportunity.

After many trials and tribulations, I finally got out of my 9- by 12-foot room and tentatively ventured out into the world again. At a support group for visually impaired people, I met a legally blind lady named Kathy Harper. She worked for the best law firm in our city, was a single mom learning to deal with low vision, and took a huge risk to join me as we launched the company now known as the Narrative Television Network.

At NTN, we help the 13 million blind and visually impaired Americans and millions more around the world access movies and television. Through our relationship with the U.S. Department of Education, we are able to make educational programming accessible for blind and visually impaired students throughout America.

Out of my own problem, I learned that there was an opportunity. The problem did not present itself as an opportunity. I could have just as easily looked at the problem and learned that my future was hopeless, helpless, and presented no possibilities. Every time we learn a lesson, we have a choice as to how we interpret, internalize, and apply the information.

We had an amazingly steep learning curve during the formation of the Narrative Television Network. We had no background, experience, expertise, or contacts in the television or movie industry, but we had learned there was an opportunity, and we knew we could learn everything else needed to solve our problem and serve others through our new business.

The very talented and skilled people who work at NTN today in our offices and studios have learned how to take a visual world on a TV or movie screen and make it verbal so blind people can hear what they can't see. This requires a unique thought process as people with sight invariably take their sight for granted and process visual information around them without any conscious effort.

I have written over 40 books and have become a bestselling author with my various titles being translated into several dozen languages, but the most difficult writing I have ever done involves taking visual images and describing them for blind people within a brief eight- or ten-second gap between the dialogue in a TV show, movie, or educational program.

Every lesson, image, or bit of information presents something we can learn. There are a myriad of possibilities in each learning opportunity. Every fact that presents itself to us can be viewed from many angles, be perceived as positive or negative, and can offer us either problems or possibilities.

The Narrative Television Network and the field of accessibility we pioneered has grown. Today, most primetime programming on major networks, first-run movies, and thousands of educational videos are fully accessible to millions of blind and visually impaired people and their families. This dream has become a reality because a problem presented itself as a learning opportunity, and we chose to view it as a path filled with potential and great possibilities.

Every time we learn something, we have a choice. I'm reminded of the two shoe salesmen who were sent to a remote South Sea island in the late 1800s. After a long voyage, the two salesmen took their shoe samples and headed to opposite ends of the island to offer their wares to the natives.

Within a week, the home office of the shoe company back in America received two telegrams. One said, "The natives here do not wear shoes. There is no opportunity for us, and I will be returning home shortly." The other telegram read, "The natives here don't wear shoes. This is the most glorious opportunity I have ever seen. Please forward all available inventory as there is tremendous potential here." Both salesmen were presented with the same information and learning opportunity, but they interpreted the facts differently, and their interpretations made all the difference.

We have learned that your mind is among the most powerful forces in the universe, but it is controlled by what you feed it. This control is based on what you choose to learn about and what interpretation or perception you glean from the information.

Success in any endeavor is a matter of following the leader. I believe in the concept I call my *Dream Team*. This involves finding individuals I admire in the various fields I am pursuing and emulating them.

When we launched the Narrative Television Network, I wanted to learn all I could, so I sought out great innovators and leaders in the industry. Ted Turner was one such individual who became a part of my Dream Team. An important part of my learning process was to determine what Mr. Turner had done to be successful, what current resources he was learning from, and what impressions and possibilities he took away from all that he was learning.

In the financial industry, people like Steve Forbes became an important part of my Dream Team, and when my books began being made as movies, I sought out people I wanted to learn from such as James Garner, Peter Fonda, Raquel Welch, Michael Landon Jr., and Academy Award-winner Louis Gossett Jr. If you are hungry to learn, you will find that the most successful people in the world are willing to share their secrets either in person or via books, articles, videos, and other resources.

All of us have our own perspectives, opinions, and bias. We must take this into account any time we are involved in learning; therefore, the first step in learning about the whole world is to learn about ourselves.

CHAPTER SIX

WHAT IS INVOLVED IN LEARNING?

RAY H. HULL, PHD

LEARNING

"The Learning Process" defines learning as a change in behavior as a result of experience.[1] I, as the author of this chapter, define learning as the acquisition of knowledge either as a result of formal learning by way of a teacher and classroom, or acquisition of new knowledge through reading or learning by imitation, e.g. learning to dance, experiences outside of a formal learning environment, or via computer.

As I will say later in this chapter, the ability to learn is not necessarily a human experience alone. Dogs learn many things during their lifetime. Mice can learn to run a maze. But, there are differences in how dogs, mice, and humans learn. To define learning in *us*, it is necessary to analyze what happens to the individual—an individual's way of thinking and feeling may change as a result of a learning experience. Everyone learns differently. The process of learning is different for everyone. But what is involved in learning? Here is a historical account that the reader may find interesting.

EARLY THEORIES OF LEARNING

Hammond, Auston, Orcutt and Rosso[2] have written a wonderful treatise on early theories of learning. In their treatise, they describe theories beginning as early as Socrates (469–300 BC), Plato (427–347), and Aristotle (384–322). Their theories were primarily concentrating on how to encourage learning, rather than the definition of learning per se. For example, Socrates taught through what he termed "dialectics"—the process of discourse and reflection.

The many theories described by Hammond include those of the Romans, which emphasized vocational training. And, when the Roman Catholic Church began to grow in Europe, the church became a primary place for learning, including universities in the twelfth century. Memorization and recitation of scripture and learning a trade was emphasized through their system of education.

In the fifteenth through the seventeenth centuries, the Renaissance period brought the liberal arts to the forefront of education by stressing the arts and humanities, freedom of thought, and the study of human values that were not strictly religious in orientation. Those teachers included such names as Martin Luther, Copernicus, and others.

The history of early education brought forth many historically significant names, such as Rene Descartes (1596–1650), who brought back the concepts of Plato and the probability of innate knowledge in children. He influenced the field of psychology with his theory of "reflex action." His theory regarding innate knowledge led to his thoughts on how the environment and the mind influence behavior. John Locke (1632–1704) was one who revived the theory of learning originally conceptualized by Aristotle. He surmised that the young mind comes into the world as a blank slate and is shaped by the child's experiences, and that it creates simple ideas from experience and then, from those experiences, develops more complex thoughts and ideas.

Hammond moves on to theorists such as Jean-Jacques Rousseu (1712–1778), who suggested that the process of education should be shaped to the individual child and that children should be allowed to develop "naturally." Immanuel Kant (1724–1804) was an early theorist who recognized cognition as an important element in learning and included cognition as the basis for the "thinking process" and the development of thoughts.

These theories, particularly those of Rousseau, then led to many other learning theories by well-known researchers such as Thorndike, Skinner, Piaget, Vygotsky, Montessori, and others.

In reviewing theories of the process of learning, it is a wonder that anyone will discover exactly how learning takes place. The many theories when looked at in their totality appear to include:

- Structured experiences

- Disciplinary modes of inquiry

- Understanding the needs of the learner

- Free expression

- Moving children away from their desks

- Learning is a developmental cognitive process.

- Students construct knowledge rather than receive knowledge.

- People learn through a trial and error approach to knowledge.

- All learning occurs in a cultural context involving social interactions.[3]

WHAT IS LEARNING?

All of the theories of learning that have been developed over the past 2,000 years have given us reason to think about the process of learning and to consider various avenues that may encourage learning.

But, in the end, what is "learning"? I finally looked up the term *learning* in the *Merriam-Webster Dictionary* to find their definition. It is as follows: "to gain knowledge, understanding, or skill by study or experience." I like that definition. Of all of the theories of learning that I have run across while authoring this chapter, that definition seems to be the most reasonable. It certainly beats, "all learning occurs in a cultural context involving social interactions," which made absolutely no sense to me.

According to an article that I read entitled, "The Learning Process," I found the following: "Learning is a change in a person's ability to behave in certain ways."

I think a better statement would have been, "Learning results in a change or expansion of a person's knowledge." People can learn in a classroom or around the dinner table, formally or informally.

The environment for learning doesn't really matter. It can happen anywhere. I gained more successful knowledge about growing dahlias from my friend Bruce Wiggin while we sat at a local bar drinking beer than from reading my many gardening books or magazines.

Thorndike, one of the many learning theorists mentioned earlier, in his treatise entitled, "The Fundamentals of Learning" presents his six laws of learning as follows, and I quote:

> 1.   *The law of readiness*: A person can learn why physically and mentally he or she is ready to respond to instruction.

> 2.   *The law of exercise*: Learning is an active process that exercises both the mind and the body. Through this process, the learner develops an adequate response to instruction and is able to master the learning through repetition.

> 3.   *The law of effect*: Learning is most effective when it is accompanied by or results in a feeling of satisfaction, pleasantness, or reward (internal or external) for the student.

4.   *The law of association*: In the learning process, the learner compares the new knowledge with his or her existing knowledge base.

5.   *The law of recency*: Practice makes perfect, and the more recent the practice, the more effective the performance of the new skill or behavior.

6.   *The law of intensity*: Real-life experiences are more likely to produce permanent behavioral changes, making this type of learning very effective."[4]

WHEN DOES LEARNING BECOME INTERESTING OR REWARDING?

Learning does not occur if it is forced, required, or mandated. We might memorize a list of requirements for job safety, for example, if it is mandated for an examination in order to maintain our job. On the other hand, we would more readily learn that list of requirements if we had just witnessed an accident that could have been avoided if we knew the contents of that list! Otherwise, it may not be something that we felt was important at the moment or something that we really wanted to learn right then—maybe later.

When does learning become interesting? It becomes interesting when it involves something we want to learn about, something that we have been looking forward to, something that we have discovered that we might find to be interesting, or something that may promote advancement in our place of employment. For example, let us say that you noticed an announcement on the bulletin board where you work that describes the potential for an upgrade and salary increase if you take advantage of a learning opportunity that will be offered online. It is only offered online, so that means engaging in an advanced learning opportunity in the evening via computer at home. You really don't want to continue working at home when you have been at work all day, but the potential upgrade in your position is important, and so you tell your employer that you are going to take advantage of the learning opportunity.

So now, your name has been placed on the list of those seeking job advancement, and you are on your way to not only learning new information but the potential for the reward of advancement and an increase in salary.

Or, perhaps away from your job you happened to see a television program that shows a fly fisher wading in a beautiful quiet lake at sunset, gracefully arcing a fly fishing rod out over the water and gently dropping a fly on the surface. Suddenly, a beautiful rainbow trout grabs the fly, and the fisher dips a hand-held net into the water and captures the fish. You are intrigued by the lovely scene, and the peaceful serenity that it evokes in your mind.

So, you decide that fly fishing might be something interesting to learn about. Therefore, the next day you take a little time to go the local library or to Google on your office computer, or perhaps even go to a video store to purchase or rent a video on that potentially interesting and relaxing sport.

That is when learning becomes interesting! The two instances above are motivating and potentially rewarding—one relative to the potential for a job upgrade and increase in salary and the other potentially rewarding because of the possibility of relaxation and experiencing the beauty of nature.

SO, WHAT IS LEARNING?

An interesting quote by Ronald E. Osborn comes to mind. It is: "Unless you try to do something beyond what you have already mastered, you will never grow." I have observed the opposite of the intent of Osborn's message in many people. Every day throughout their working years they faithfully go to work, they do their job, go home, have dinner, watch TV for a while, and then go to bed. The next day, they get out of bed and do the same thing. And their life goes on and on and on.

Their job has become something that they do by rote memory—no creativity, nothing new learned, they just do their job and go home. Why? It is probably because they have not searched for new adventure, new knowledge, new and interesting avenues to venture into. Or, perhaps new avenues for learning have presented themselves to the person, but she or he either ignored them or might have thought about them and then allowed them to pass by without determining if they might have been interesting enough to learn more about.

In 1956, Benjamin Bloom identified three types, or categories, of learning, referred to as *Bloom's Taxonomy of Learning*—the categories, or domains, in which learning takes place.[5] Those are:

- Cognitive domain—knowledge

- Psychomotor domain—physical use of knowledge

- Affective domain—attitudes, emotions, or values

I am going to discuss the first two—the cognitive and psychomotor learning domains.

COGNITIVE LEARNING

Cognitive learning is described in *Bloom's Taxonomy* as the process of learning by instruction and requires the following:

- Remembering what has been learned in the past

- Comprehension—understanding the information

- Application—using the information

- Analysis—breaking the information into understandable parts

- Synthesis—integrating the information into a usable whole

- Evaluation—using standards to judge the worth of the information

In other words, cognitive learning involves the standard process of learning and using facts—principles that were, perhaps, learned in school. Most importantly, however, it involves applying the information that we have learned to our job, our new recreational interest, the new instrument that we are learning to play, or any other aspect of our life where learning applies.

PSYCHOMOTOR LEARNING

This form of learning involves the use of the brain and one's senses to tell the body what to do. As in the cognitive domain, the phases of learning build progressively, one upon the other. According to *Bloom's Taxonomy*, those six levels are as follows:

- Observation—watching the skill or activity being performed. That is, for example, generally how we learn to dance, throw a line into the water for fly fishing, or put paper into a copy machine so it doesn't jam.

- Imitation—copying the skill or activity in a step-by-step manner.

- Manipulation—performing the skill based on instruction.

- Precision—performing the skill or activity until it becomes a habit.

- Articulation—combining multiple skills.

- Naturalization—performing multiple skills correctly consistently

So in *Bloom's Taxonomy*, psychomotor skills build on each other to consistently correct performance.

I remember when I took lessons in tap dancing. I was 12 years of age and had never danced before. My mother thought it would help my stuttering and also might help me to become more graceful. When I went to my first lesson, my teacher showed me where she wanted me to be, skill-wise, when I became a good tap dancer. When I observed her grace and agility while engaging in those complicated tap dance steps, I just knew that I would never be able to reach that level of skill! But, then we began the first basic tap dance steps.

Tap—tap tap, tap—tap tap, tap—tap tap; slowly and laboriously I took those first tap dance steps.

After that first lesson, I went home with my tap dance shoes, taps on the toes and heels, and walked out to my father's milk barn and onto the concrete floor where the cows were milked twice a day. The open milk parlor and the clean, smooth, concrete floor were just perfect for tap dancing! The taps sounded loud and the walls echoed to the sounds of my tap shoes. When I went tap—tap tap, tap—tap tap, it sounded great! Just like Gene Kelly in the movie *Singing in the Rain*! I thought, "Wow! I'm good!" From that time on, every week when I went to my tap dance lessons, I kept improving until I reached the level (or near it) that my teacher showed me on that first day of class!

So, learning in the psychomotor domain by imitation, manipulation, and precision worked! I had learned to tap dance! It happened because I watched, I imitated, and eventually by combining multiple skills—my arms, my body positioning, the movements of my head, and the movements of my legs and feet—I became a very good tap dancer! So...what is the goal of learning?

THE GOAL OF LEARNING

Wirth and Perkins say something that I feel is quite profound:

> If you ask most college teachers what is the greatest gift they could give their students,

you will rarely hear an answer that includes mention of specific discipline-related content. [In other words, they usually do not mention student achievements in math, physics, English, or the specific subject matter for which they are responsible.] Most will answer, "the desire and skills for life-long learning." It's not that it isn't important to learn some facts while in college; these will likely be necessary for future employment. More important though is having the skill to learn on one's own after leaving college. This single, most-important skill will empower for a lifetime and should be one of your highest priorities.[6]

SIGNIFICANT LEARNING

Going beyond *Bloom's Taxonomy*, Dr. L. Dee Fink desired a broader definition of learning that involved changes in the learner. He called it *significant learning* that involves "some kind of lasting change that is important in terms of the learner's life."[7] According to Fink, there are three levels of learning. Those include:

1. **Foundational Knowledge**: This involves understanding basic facts, ideas, and perspectives. It involves understanding the basic facts of a subject so

that they can be applied to other areas of knowledge.

2. **Application of Knowledge**: Beyond understanding the basic facts of a subject, the learner also needs to know how to apply the knowledge that has been gained, engaging in new levels of thinking and learning new skills.

3. **Integration of Knowledge**: Fink says that real knowledge involves integration of information, connecting what has been learned with other knowledge, and being able to use the knowledge in one's life. One then learns the reason for gaining knowledge in a specific area. We become an *intentional learner* because we *want* to learn about a certain subject that interests us.

BECOMING AN INTENTIONAL LEARNER

Becoming an intentional learner means "developing self-awareness about the reason for study, the learning process itself, and how education is used." Intentional learners are integrative thinkers who "see connections in seemingly disparate information" to inform their decisions. Self-directed learners are highly motivated, independent, and strive toward self-direction and autonomy. They "take the initiative to diagnose their learning needs, formulate learning goals, identify resources for learning, select an implement learning strategies, and evaluate learning outcomes (Savin-Baden and Major 2004)."[8]

But, in order to become an intentional learner, one must *want* to learn, and for that to happen the subject must be interesting to the person. As I said earlier in this chapter, whether the intentional learner happened to see a segment on television about snow skiing, fly fishing, or learning to play the accordion—or for the math enthusiast, learning a new form of mathematical calculation—a spark of interest to learn more about the subject may have been lit. So the next step is the local library, the video store, or Google to find out more about the subject.

A friend of mine happened to see a segment in National Geographic magazine that showed beautiful photographs of scenery and people. Those photographs so intrigued her that she started looking for books on photography. She became an avid reader about that subject to the extent that she went to a camera store and bought a good camera and some lenses that would allow for some photographic creations that she wanted to try. She then enrolled in a course in photography at a local community college and began taking evening classes on that subject, which included scenic and professional photography of people.

As a result of the extensive reading that she continued to engage in on the subject of photography and the formal courses that she was taking, she eventually decided on a career change to professional photography. She seemed to have a knack for taking excellent photographs of people, so she leased a small space in a strip mall and opened a photography studio with the intent to engage in portrait photography. In light of her learned skill in photographing scenery and people, she became a sought-after photographer for weddings, graduation photographs, and others that combined the use of outdoor scenery and excellent portrait photography of people of all ages.

So, intentional learning for this woman paid off in a successful career in photography! I didn't become a professional tap dancer, but during high school and college I was a sought-after dance performer for stage productions and was a member of a dance team that performed for many occasions. I wasn't a professional performer, but I had fun and made a little money for various performances!

ONE MORE LEARNING THEORY

There are so many theories of learning—some traditional, others that seem logical in their approach, and others we hear little about. For example, there is some discussion about whether it is best to learn in group environments or individually. I don't do well in group learning environments—too much discussion, too much competiveness, too many distractions. However, I was reading the other day about a theory of learning called the *Collaborative Learning Model*. The title of article was, "Supporting Social Interaction in an Intelligent Collaborative Learning System."[9] As I read that article, it led me to remembering one of my significant learning experiences.

That model of learning is one I can identify with. When I was in college, the young lady to whom I was most attracted was an excellent student. I thought that she was not only beautiful, but she was intelligent, outgoing, and was the model student her professors wished everyone would emulate. Up to that time, I had been, to say the least, an average student. I studied only what I felt I had to study and spent more time being in plays and musicals than in the classroom. The young lady whom I sought after seemed to not even be aware that I existed, let alone be a young man to whom she might be attracted.

As time passed, realizing more and more that I was making no progress in getting her interested in me I began to think that perhaps if I was more like her, a star student, maybe she would be more attracted to me. So, I began to study harder. My time in the library was taken seriously, and my reason for being there went beyond "girl watching" to actually learning the material for the courses I was taking that semester. I began to become known as a serious student. I even asked the young lady who was the impetus for the change in my attitude regarding scholarship if we could study together from time to time. To my surprise, she said yes! After a while, our Wednesday evening study time became a regular event!

If one is looking for an example of the *social interaction model* of learning, I suppose that the previous story is one of those. Of course there are other examples that could have been shared, but that one has a happy outcome!

SUMMARY TO THE CHAPTER

In summary of this chapter, we must remember that the ability to learn is one of the most outstanding characteristics of being human. As I said earlier in this chapter, learning occurs continuously throughout one's lifetime. But, in order to define learning, per se, it is necessary to analyze what happens to the learner when learning is taking place. For example, as a result of a learning experience, a person's way of perceiving, thinking, feeling, and doing may change. The learning experience may involve complex intellectual or attitudinal changes that can affect behavior in subtle ways.

But, to clearly define "learning" is nearly impossible. You can ask the question, "What is learning?" "When does learning occur?" "What is involved in learning?"

We may think that we can answer those questions, but then we will find that one universal answer is not enough. In all of the reading and preparation that I have engaged in as I write this chapter, I have come to one conclusion: literally hundreds of people have written and published theories about the process of learning, but none of them have actually accomplished the task.

I have come to the conclusion that learning, per se, cannot be defined. Everyone learns differently. Therefore, the process of learning is different for everyone. This is something that teachers and parents need to learn too. I wish that I could have told my teachers that when I was in grade school, high school, and college!

NOTES

1. "The Learning Process," Dynamic Flight, November 11, 2003, http://www.dynamicflight. com/avcfibook/learning_process/.

2. Linda Darling-Hammond et al., *How People Learn: Introduction to Learning Theory*, Stanford University, Learner.org, 2001, 12-13, accessed July 2, 2017, https://www.learner.org/courses/ learningclassroom/support/01_intro.pdf.

3. Ibid.

4. Ibid.

5. Benjamin Bloom, *Taxonomy of Educational Objectives* (Boston, MA: Allyn and Bacon/ Pearson Education, 1984).

6. Karl R. Wirth and Dexter Perkins, *Learning to Learn*, Macalester College, September 16, 2008, https://www.macalester.edu/academics/geology/wirth/learning.pdf.

7. L. See Fink, Creating Significant Learning Experiences: An Integrated Approach to Designing College Courses (San Francisco, CA: Jossey-Bass Publishers, 2003).

8. Wirth and Perkins, *Learning to Learn*.

9. Amy Soller, "Supporting Social Interaction in an Intelligent Collaborative Learning System," *International Journal of Artificial Intelligence in Education* 12 (2001): 40-62.

CHAPTER SEVEN

LIVING TO LEARN

JIM STOVALL

The highest utilization of learning is to apply knowledge and wisdom in our lives in productive ways. Productivity is the pursuit of creating more efficiency and results in all that we do, especially as we are serving others.

For over a decade, I have studied productivity, and this research culminated in a book entitled *The Art of Productivity*. In that book, I offered my readers the opportunity to take an assessment and get a Productivity Profile of their strengths and preferences relating to motivation, communication, and implementation. You can receive your own Productivity Profile at www. UltimateProductivity.com using the code 586404. Discovering our own strengths and preferences is the key to productively implementing everything that we learn.

If we are going to understand and apply our learning in productive ways that make a true difference, we must master motivation, communication, and implementation. All learning is valid and legitimate, but some learning is more productive given that we all have individual goals, dreams, and aspirations.

When I was in grade school, I learned the capitals of all 50 states. As I sit here dictating the words you are reading, I still remember that Pierre is the capital of South Dakota. I have traveled several million miles in my life and have never been to Pierre or even South Dakota.

Often when I give speeches overseas and my words are being translated into other languages, I memorize the opening of my remarks or at least a greeting in the language of my audience. While I have memorized the words and can repeat them, I haven't really learned them. In order to determine what type of learning is most productive, we must understand where we are trying to go and what goals we want to reach.

Motivation is the key to learning, and learning is the key to staying motivated. None of us succeed in any endeavor on our own. Collaboration is the key to success. This gives me the perfect opportunity to recognize some valuable colleagues who have made this book possible. None of my 40 books would exist, including the one you're reading now, without my in-house editor, grammarian, and colleague to whom I am dictating these words, Dorothy Thompson. This book is more valid, impactful, and accurate thanks to my esteemed coauthor, Dr. Raymond Hull. And without David Wildasin and his team at Sound Wisdom Publishing, you would never have received this book. Collaboration dictates that we must understand our own motivation, the motivation of those around us, and be able to internalize it all. We must learn what motivates us and be able to teach it to others.

It took me years to learn that just because something motivates me, doesn't mean that it motivates anyone else. Some people are motivated by recognition, money, acclaim, inclusion, or self-actualization. If you learn what motivates those around you, you can create a collaborative effort in which they are pursuing their passions as you pursue your own.

It's not always easy to understand the motivations of others. I remember getting on an early-morning flight to travel to a speaking engagement as often happens in my world. This particular day, the gate agents were polite and enthusiastic, the baggage handlers seemed motivated, and all of the other airline personnel seemed to be on their best behavior. This is not always the case, particularly on an early-morning flight.

As a blind person myself, I'm allowed to pre-board flights, so as I got onto the plane and settled into my seat, I became aware that there was only one other person on the plane, and they were sitting right across the aisle from me. I put out my hand and offered a greeting. "Hello. I'm Jim Stovall." The person across the aisle shook my hand warmly and told me his name, and I instantly realized I was shaking hands with the president of the airline. I immediately knew why all the airline staff and personnel were polite and fully engaged.

The flight attendants were particularly attentive, and at one point during the flight the president of the airline asked them how they liked his new incentive bonus plan. The flight attendants standing in the aisle gushed forth their praise and adulation for him and his wonderful plan.

Later in that flight, I got up to use the restroom and passed by the galley where the flight attendants were preparing our meal. I clearly overheard one of them mutter, "Can you believe that idiot thinks we're motivated by his ridiculous plan?"

The other flight attendant remarked, "Not only am I not motivated, I'm insulted."

When I returned to my seat, I pondered the fact that the president of that airline sitting right across the aisle from me knew less about what would motivate his colleagues than I did.

Assuming you understand other people without taking the time and effort to learn about them is a form of prejudice. Prejudice is a lazy mental exercise. If you know what motivates yourself, you can pursue your passion and learn everything necessary to rise to the top of any field.

One of the best aspects of a formal education is that you become aware of all the things that there are to learn about. People get doctoral degrees in many areas of study that I didn't even know existed until I went to college.

One of the amazing benefits of reading a book a day is that I am constantly learning about more people, places, and things I want to study. Once you discover what motivates you and the people around you and you start learning what it takes to be successful in your particular area, you must learn to communicate.

Communication is the key to all formal and informal learning. As we learned in a previous chapter, we should never take advice from anybody who doesn't have what we want. In much the same way, we must be careful what we learn and who we learn it from. The

Internet is an amazing learning and communication tool, but we must be able to discern the validity and accuracy of what we are learning.

Just as we discovered that there are a number of learning differences or preferences, people communicate most effectively in different ways. The best communication is two-way communication. It must be open, consistent, and free-flowing.

Jimi Hendrix has been quoted as saying, "Knowledge speaks, but wisdom listens."

I work with a variety of people who communicate in different ways. Some people are verbal while others prefer written communications. Some people need to see something or visualize it to understand it while others need to repeat what they're understanding back to whomever is communicating with them. Some people learn or communicate best experientially.

For almost 20 years, I've had an ongoing relationship with a wonderful training company called Klemmer and Associates. They teach life and success principles through a series of exercises and real-world experiences. I've observed amazing results from their work, and a number of people who have gone through their training tell me they've read many books and attended numerous lectures, but until they experienced it, they couldn't really learn it.

As a blind person, I experience my own form of learning differences and communication preferences.

There is a particular West Coast resort hotel I have been to over 40 times to give corporate speeches. The staff at this particular property is very attentive and contacted me with an alternative method to communicate my phone messages to me. They never asked me what I would prefer nor explored how to communicate with a blind person, so I wasn't surprised when chaos ensued.

On one memorable trip, the resort manager welcomed me at the front desk and told me how much they appreciated all of my stays at their property. He went on to explain that he knew that, as a blind person, I couldn't see the red light on the phone that lit up when I had phone messages, so he and his team had come up with an alternative way to communicate with me.

I was obviously very appreciative of their consideration and effort until he explained, "From now on, whenever you have a phone message come in to the switchboard, our operator will write it on a slip of paper and give it to the bellman who will deliver all your phone message slips to your room and slide them under the door. That way, when you return to your room after your speech, you will have all your phone messages."

To this day, I have never understood why he and his team thought phone messages written on slips of paper would be more visible to me than a red light blinking on the telephone. Never assume you have communicated, and never assume that someone has learned what you are teaching.

One of the worst questions you can ever ask anyone is "Do you understand?" Everyone who misunderstands what you're teaching or communicating thinks they understand, so when you ask, "Do you understand?" they will invariably reply, "Yes." This results in false learning and miscommunication. The most powerful question you can ask is, "What do you understand?" When the answer to that question resembles what you are teaching or communicating, you have succeeded.

Once you have learned about your own motivation and communication preferences, as well as the preferences of those around you, you are ready to apply the final step in productive learning, which is implementation. Learning, like anything else we do regularly, will become a habit.

Anything you do for 21 days in a row will begin to insert itself into your subconscious. This means that after 21 days of doing something, if you don't do it on the following day, it will seem unfamiliar and uncomfortable. I have read a book a day via high-speed audio for over 20 years. On rare occasions when illness or scheduling keeps me from my reading, I feel out of sorts as if something is amiss.

Whatever goals you decide to pursue in your personal and professional life, constant learning will be the cornerstone of your future success.

People implement tasks, including learning, in all manner of ways. Some people multitask while others implement in a linear fashion, completing one project before they move to the next. Some people need to work as part of a team while others need to work alone and then bring their component of the job to the finished product.

Learning without an outlet or application is unproductive. We all know people who seem to collect college degrees. They enjoy the process of learning, which is valid and to be applauded, but unless we apply that which we have learned in the real world we can never make the impact that we are intended to make throughout our lives.

Implementing, sharing, and teaching that which we have learned does not diminish us. Knowledge is a commodity, but it is not like any other commodity. If you possess gold, oil, or money and share it with those around you, you will have less, and they will have more. If you share information, knowledge, or wisdom with others, they will have more, and you will find yourself elevated in every way.

You must study your passion and be passionate about all that you study. Constantly revisit the books and other learning resources that have impacted you the most. No matter how many times you have reviewed a great book, you will find hidden treasures when you reread it again.

Memory is like a muscle. You either use it or lose it. For many years, my father ran a retirement center and nursing home, so I visited the facility countless times and met many of the residents. I learned that people in their 80s, 90s, or even over 100 who continue to learn stay vital, alert, and relevant. Those people who stop learning and pursuing knowledge begin to waste away both mentally and physically.

In our society, we have made the mistake of using some of the best elements around us as punishment. Whether it's vegetables, exercise, or learning, both children and adults should understand and embrace that vegetables are good as well as good for us, exercise is fun as well as healthy, and learning is both productive and profitable.

Too often, kids who have misbehaved are forced to read a book and write a report. It's no wonder many students in our schools aren't engaged in learning. In their minds, learning has become a punishment, not the key to success, happiness, and enlightenment.

Deconstruction is a principal I have developed that has become a valuable tool in learning as well as every area of my life. It's easy to get caught up in what we want to have, who we want to be, and what we want to do. While this process of projecting into the future can be useful, it's also important to examine who we are, what we have, and what we do now.

This learning comes through the process of deconstruction, which involves approaching every area of our lives with the simple question, "Why?" If you look at why you have the job you have, why you work in the field you work in, why you live in the area where you live, why you have the friends and associates you have, and all other similar questions, you will begin to benefit from deconstruction, which takes everything back to its fundamental form.

You may look at your career path or personal life through the lens of deconstruction and determine you are where you are because it is your passion, calling, and destiny. On the other hand, you may learn through deconstruction that your career came about because you took the first part-time job you could get when you were in high school and never explored working anywhere else. You may discover your friends, colleagues, and associates are the people who feed your spirit and soul the most and support you as you pursue your destiny, or you may find that the people you hang around with were just the first folks you met when you got to town, and you never bothered to meet anyone else. Recent psychological research has revealed that you become like, assume the attitudes of, and earn the average income of the five people you spend the most time with.

Learning this should cause us all to choose wisely those with whom we invest our time. In much the same way, you can learn from comic books, college texts, tabloid publications, or romance novels. All can be valid learning tools at the right time and in the proper proportion.

Without fail, what we learn will impact who we are and who we will become, so we must control our learning as we fully understand that our learning will control us.

CHAPTER EIGHT

LEARNING IS A NEVER-ENDING ADVENTURE

RAY H. HULL, PHD

"The greatest lesson I have learned in life is that I still have a lot to learn."

—AUTHOR UNKNOWN

Brett and Kate McKay wrote in "How and Why to Become a Lifelong Learner" that if one goes beyond their formal education, which takes about twenty-two years of spending our time in classrooms learning new things, wonderful things will happen![1] But, just because we have concluded our formal education doesn't mean that our education is over.

Edward Paxton Hood, in a brief treatise written in 1852 entitled *Self-Education: Twelve Chapters for Young Thinkers*, states:

> Our whole life is an Education—we are "ever-learning," every moment of time, everywhere, under all circumstances something is being added to the stock of our previous attainments. Mind is always at work when once its operations commence. All [people] are learners, whatever their occupation, in the palace, in the cottage, in the park, and the field. These are the laws stamped upon Humanity.[2]

WHY BECOME A LIFELONG LEARNER?

What occurs if we continue to learn? Brett and Kate McKay continue by listing "Why" as follows:

You'll earn more. Fifty or sixty years ago, you could finish college and you'd have all the education you needed for the rest of your career. You don't have that luxury in today's job market.

You'll be more interesting and charismatic. Those who met Theodore Roosevelt were always impressed with his ability to hold a conversation with anyone regarding any subject imaginable. ...How did Theodore Roosevelt become such a charismatic, conversational dynamo? ...While in the White House, he would read a book every day before breakfast. If he didn't have any official business in the evening, he would read two or three more books, plus any magazines and newspapers that caught his fancy. ...As a result, he could connect with anyone, from any walk of life, on something that truly interested the other person.

You'll be a better leader. Being able to connect with others doesn't just make you more interesting. It also makes you more influential. The greater your knowledge base, the more you can meet people where they are, and the greater the stockpile of solutions you have at your disposal to tackle problems and overcome challenges.

You'll be independent and handy. [It's great to be independent and handy. At our house, whenever something breaks or otherwise needs repairs, I have to call a repair person to come out and fix it.]

Lifelong learning keeps your brain healthy. Henry Ford said, "Anyone who stops learning is old, whether twenty or eighty. Anyone who keeps learning stays young."[3]

"But it's not just learning that's important. It's learning what to do with what you learn and learning why you learn at all that matters."[4] We must keep our mind young in order to think young! An "old" mind is one that has not continued to learn. Continuing to learn can ward off a deteriorating brain that can lead to dementia.

WE ARE ALWAYS LEARNING

Michael Bond states that "You are always learning and discovering new things that will allow you to continue on the path of success. Everyone is always in motion at some time in their life."[5] The world is always changing, and if we don't improve, we will be left behind.

Mrs. Hamilton was my teacher at my two-room country school. In her classroom were four grades—the fifth, sixth, seventh and eighth grades. There were three of us in my fifth grade class. She not only taught us what was in our textbooks, but she taught us much beyond that. We learned about the world, we learned about things we had never seen, things that went beyond our classroom activities and textbook learning experiences.

Mrs. Hamilton taught us to go beyond our country school, to learn about the world beyond that rather remote location. She brought us sea shells from Hawaii, she brought us a pomegranate to taste, she brought us souvenirs from Mexico, she gave each of us a jar of earth, gave us a seed, and asked us to plant it in the dirt in the jar and sit it by the school house window so we could see the roots begin to grow and then the plant emerge from the earth as the leaves would begin to stretch forth, and many more experiences about the world. Mrs. Hamilton taught us to go beyond our text books and learn about many things. Mrs. Hamilton probably wasn't thinking about those experiences in this way, but in one way or another she was preparing the children in her classroom to become lifelong learners, to continue to explore the world and learn about new things!

Ravi Sankar Venna says:

> Continuous learning is a process which is surrounded by your attitude to learn and share the knowledge, academic curiosity, reading and practicing, creativity, thinking ability.... Many people once they passed any certification or attained a degree, they would feel that they have achieved the pinnacle of life. However, in reality, it is not. It is only a small part in the life long learning process.[6]

Sankar Venna continues by saying that there are many ways that we can learn on a continuous basis. He lists some as follows:

1. **On-the-Job Experience**: He says that on-the-job experience is an effective way of learning and gaining new knowledge. If you give your best in your work and continue to add to your knowledge base, your experiences will help you attain real learning.

2. **Reading**: The gains that you experience through reading are one of the best ways to expand your learning base. If you have some free time, you become better by engaging in productive reading. If you learn one new thing from reading, then you can eventually master a subject that you are interested in.

3. **Teaching and Mentoring**: We learn best by teaching others. It helps us establish or reestablish our knowledge base on our subject matter. However, mentoring does not need to be restricted to a specific form of subject matter. It can include guiding others, directing, advising, and motivating people around us. When people begin to realize our

knowledge and abilities, it can be a great start to a new journey in life.[7]

Never stop learning, because life never stops teaching!

IF WE STOP LEARNING, OUR LIFE, OUR JOB WILL REMAIN AT A STANDSTILL

We should never complete our education. I know that once we graduate it becomes easy to say to ourselves, "Now I'm done! I know all that I need to know to succeed in life!" But in reality, that is not the case. The world will pass us by if that is where we remain. The field that we are in will pass us by. We need to have the fortitude to continue to learn. I, personally, have found that if I let a few months pass by without keeping up with the technology that is available in my field, it takes more time than that to learn what I need to know in order to at least remain current, let alone get ahead in regard to what it takes to serve my patients in an expert manner. And that is not in my field alone. I'm speaking here about all fields, unless the shovel that you are using to dig pipe trenches continues to work for you.

Here are a few advantages to keeping up with new advancements in our fields.

1. We can raise our income by being at the top of the ladder in regard to the technology needed to serve our clients in the most advanced manner. My physician colleagues advance their knowledge by attending seminars

and continuing education sessions to learn about the newest advances in the use of laser technology and other systems that are necessary to best serve their patients. I am required to obtain a minimum of 30 continuing education hours each year in order to maintain my license to practice in my field. And, along with obtaining additional hours advancing my knowledge, my income increases because I can add to the services that I offer.

Some businesses give automatic raises to employees who engage in advanced learning through continuing education. That is incentive enough to engage in additional learning experiences so that those opportunities for advancement do not pass us by!

2. The satisfaction of knowing that we are, indeed, not letting the world pass us by is absolutely worthwhile! By continuing to learn, we are keeping up with new information or regaining information that we may have learned in the past but need to recoup in order to move forward. We increase our vocabulary, we increase our social standing, we simply become more knowledgeable about subjects that we may find most interesting. We don't allow our mind to become stagnant, to become dull. We remain bright, involved, and engaged with the world around us!

BECOMING A LIFELONG LEARNER

"You can't teach an old dog new tricks." I'm sure that you have heard that old adage. Well, that old saying doesn't apply to people, and I'm not even sure whether it applies to dogs! We can all learn, even into great ages. Some of the greatest authors and composers are in their 80s and 90s. Tony Bennet, the great popular, vocalist is in his middle nineties, and he is still learning and composing new music for performances and travels all around the U.S. and other countries singing in concerts to sold-out crowds.

Here are some suggestions for becoming a lifelong learner:

1. We must adjust our concept of learning.

As I said earlier in this chapter, learning doesn't have to take place in a classroom. I grew up on a farm in the middle of Kansas. You cannot find a more stereotypical rural setting than that. As long as I lived on that farm between college and graduate school, I was responsible for three of our hired hands in one way or another, making sure they were fulfilling their responsibilities and giving them their duties each day. Their names were Elmer Mowbray, A.P. Nichols, and Slim Elder.

Elmer Mowbray was an older man who typically had an unlit cigar tucked away in the corner of his mouth. He walked slowly, talked slowly, seemed to think slowly, but he was always on the job ready to lend a hand. We could always depend on Elmer to be there when we needed help with fence repairs, driving a tractor and pulling a hay wagon to pick up hay bales out in the field, or other such chores.

A. P. Nichols was also an older man—never married, lived with his sister on a neighboring farm, and worked around our farm when we needed extra help. He was a kind and gentle soul who never had a harsh word to say about anyone. Both he and Elmer had solid philosophies of life that they would tell me about from time to time. If I had a question about life, love, or sin, all I had to do was ask, and they would expound on their philosophy about it.

One day while all three of us were sitting on top of five layers of hay bales on a hay wagon as it was being pulled by my father who was driving a tractor toward the hay loft where those bales were to be stacked, I asked both of them what they thought about God. Their only response was, "That's something that we don't have to worry about. God is with us throughout every day and night of our lives. He loves us and will take us to Heaven when we die." That was it. Nothing else was mentioned. I have remembered that conversation to this day.

Slim Elder was another matter. He was around 30 years old, thin as a rail, and much taller than I was. He spoke with a slow Kansas drawl, and usually had a cigarette tucked away on top of one of his ears. One day as we were sitting in the shade by one of our out buildings on the farm waiting for a load of wheat to be brought in so we could shovel it into one of our many grain bins, I asked him if he had a girlfriend and if he knew anything about love. He perked up and said without hesitation, "Sure I have a girlfriend. She lives over by Windom (Kansas). I see her every once in a while. We're sort of going steady. Why?"

I told him that I had been dating a young lady, a Mennonite girl, and liked her a lot. I said that it feels like "love," but I don't know what love is. All Slim said was, "When it's love, you'll know it."

So then I asked him, "How will I know it?"

Slim's only reply was, "That's it. You'll know it. It's a special feeling that will tell you that it is love." That ended the conversation. I pondered what he said for some time, but all I could do was believe him. I'm not sure if he really knew what love was or if he was ever in love. But, I believed him. After all, he was over 30 years old, so he should know.

Those were learning experiences that happened on a hay wagon and in the shade of an outbuilding on our farm. They didn't happen in a classroom, or from a book, or even on Google. But they were still good learning experiences that came from good honest people and can happen once in a life time.

2. Ask Questions or Encourage Others to Question Your Ideas

One of the best ways to foster learning is to ask questions or encourage others to ask questions of us. In the situations above, I learned from our three hired hands because I asked questions about things I had wondered about. Brett and Kate McKay state that we sometimes learn best when we are in a group. When we are in a group environment—whether it is at a restaurant, at a local bar on Friday afternoon, or in a meeting when we throw out an idea that we have been thinking about—we can expect responses from those in the group. Some may be affirming, others may be questioning our logic, others may add to our idea by giving us additional information that will help solidify the concept that we have been considering. But, in one way or another, our ideas may expand into concepts, and the concepts may expand into theories, and from there into learning more than we originally expected to learn.

3. Remember That Learning Is a Continuous, Lifelong Process: Where Do I Want to Be?

> Continuous learning is a process which is surrounded by your attitude to learn and share the knowledge, academic curiosity, reading and practicing, creativity, thinking ability and extending your knowledge levels. All these are very important in making you perfect personality.[9]

But, what do you want to be? Where do you want to be in your life? All of us have skills that we have developed over time. But, what additional skills would bring us to where we want to be in our work, our life, or our relationship with others? One way of doing that is to write them down on paper, even writing them in general terms if they haven't become detailed in your mind. The skills that you would like to develop don't have to immediately be specified. Simply write down the goals that you would like to achieve down the road, even in general terms, and the skills that you will need to achieve those goals will follow naturally.

4. Everyone Is in Motion: Continuous Learning Takes Advantage of Opportunities

Michael Bond makes note of the fact that everyone is continually in motion:

> They are either going up and getting better, or they can be falling back on bad habits. Nobody is ever standing still in life. That is because the world is always changing and if you don't improve you will be left behind. Not only is the world always changing, but so are you. You are not the same person that you were last year, last month, or even yesterday. You have changed, even if it has been very little.[10]

Continuous learning means taking advantage of opportunities that either you create or someone creates for you to take advantage of. People who are successful use downtime on their job or on vacation to increase their knowledge. Reading is a good way to do that. In fact, reading is an excellent way to develop a continuous learning habit.

5. Expect to Adjust Your Course from Time to Time

As Bond states:

> When you drive a car, you are always making small adjustments and corrections while going in directions you are headed. That constant adjustment becomes very familiar and eventually you don't even realize that you are making these adjustments. This is because the road is not always totally smooth and straight. The same goes for your goals and your life. There will always be small bumps in the road of life and you will always need to make adjustments to reach your goals.[11]

If one of our goals is to complete an evening course for job advancement and a family situation arises that interferes with your completion of it at that time, you may need to make an adjustment that may require that you temporarily postpone all or part of it. You may have to adjust your destination and complete that course of study a little later than intended. It probably doesn't mean that completion of your course will be terminated, but rather simply postponed.

6. We Need to Accept the Possibility of Failure

We have to accept the possibility that attempting to achieve something—a job advancement, learning a new skill that might result in an independent business, inventing a new tool that we feel could revolutionize an aspect of manufacturing, or setting out to complete a course of study for a job advancement may not turn out the way we had hoped. We simply weren't successful in completing the task.

Henry Cloud, author of *Never Go Back: 10 Things You'll Never Do Again*, admonishes the reader to never return to the same thing, whether it be a job or a relationship that was unsuccessful. His advice: "We should never go back to the same thing expecting different results,"[12] without something being different. In other words, unless we change something within what went wrong, we should never return to the same thing.

Let us say that you entered into a course of study that was to lead to an advancement in your position within the company where you work. As the course of study began, you found it to be extremely difficult and full of information that you have never encountered before. You had a strong feeling that it is going to require more study time and more outside reading than you had time for, and you wondered if you could even complete the course of study with a passing grade.

So eventually you reluctantly withdraw, even though the money that you spent for enrollment will not be returned. You are disappointed in yourself, angry at your job that you felt interfered with your ability to complete the course, and embarrassed to tell your wife that you quit the course of study that was going to bring more income into your household. You are sad, disappointed, and angry—mostly angry at yourself for dropping out when two of your colleagues have remained to complete the course.

Pauline Estrem, in "Why Failure Is Good for Success," writes:

> The sweetest victory is the one that's most difficult. The one that requires you to reach down deep inside, to fight with everything you've got, to be willing to leave everything out there on the battlefield—without knowing, until that do-or-die moment, if your heroic effort will be enough.[13]

She says in that treatise that failures can become stepping stones to success. So, although being angry, disappointed, and embarrassed at yourself for giving up and dropping out of the course that could have led to advancement in your place of employment along with an increase in salary, you return to the instructor of the course to say that you have decided to remain in the course. You are told by the instructor that you have missed important information, and that the portion of the course that you have missed will require some extra work to catch up. But, you are determined to complete the course and complete it successfully. And you do! It was a heroic effort, as Estrem calls it, but your heroic effort was enough, and you were successful!

So, failure can also be a stepping stone to success if we have the wherewithal to rise above failure, use it as leverage, and have the courage and the drive to move forward. The problem is that there are too many people in our world who let failure determine the outcomes in their life rather than rising above and moving on. You don't make it into the history books based on your failures. You make it into the history books by overcoming failure and achieving what you intended to achieve!

If we did all the things we are capable of doing, we would literally astound ourselves.

—THOMAS EDISON

LEARNING AS A LIFELONG ADVENTURE

I guess that I should be asking a question here, "Why become a lifelong learner?" So, why not be? There are so many benefits that can develop into advantages in one's life that arise out of continuously walking along that road of adventure that it becomes ridiculous not to become one! Beside the advantage of keeping one's brain healthy, as I said in this chapter, you can earn more, you can become more charismatic and interesting, you can become a better leader, you can become more independent.

But whether we want to or not, we continue to learn. We learn something from everyone we meet; we learn something everywhere we go; if we go to church on Sunday, we learn something even though we may say we don't; if we go to a movie, we learn something. We can't help it! It happens!

As I quoted earlier in this chapter, even if we are considered an expert in our field of endeavor, there are still advancements being made in it by others, and if we don't keep up, we will be left behind. Having a college education is never enough to end one's educational life.

FALSE BARRIERS TO LEARNING[14]

Perceived barriers to lifelong learning come from people who seem to give the same excuses for not taking up lifelong learning and instead opt for a life filled with entertainment. What are the excuses? Among them include the following:

Time

Everyone is busy. It may be hard to cram time into your already busy schedule in order to continue learning. However, you don't need to spend hours every day reading or rehearsing or practicing. As I tell my patients, one of the best ways for children to develop language is to have a parent who is willing to sit down with them and look at picture books and discuss what the pictures are about. Parents tell me that they don't have time to do that. My response is that if you read to your young child for 30 minutes in the evening before she or he goes to bed, over a seven-day week that totals two and a half hours of good language stimulation!

The same goes for self-study. We don't have to think in terms of hours at a time but rather 30 to 45 minutes a day, which will total two and a half hours to five hours and fifteen minutes a week. That ends up being quite a bit of self-study time!

Money

Audiobooks are inexpensive and easy to carry with you, as are good books that can be checked out from your local library. The barrier of money exists only if you think that you must enroll at a local college or university for continue your education. Even then, some college classes do not charge tuition for adult learners. If you have to wait at the doctor's office, have a good book with you to read instead of watching waiting-room television.

Location

In my previous chapter, I mentioned that learning takes place in the least expected locations. I can learn just as much at the dinner table as I did in some of my college classes. I learned more about growing dahlias from my friend Bruce while we were having a couple of glasses of beer at a local bar than I did reading about the process in my gardening magazines. Only certain things will need a more elaborate location—learning to ski if you happen to live in Florida, for example!

WE NEED A GOAL FOR LEARNING

Again, whether we intend to or not, we are learning every day along our life adventure. But, it is good to have goals for learning. I love photography, and I am a fanatic when it comes to any new book that comes out on that topic. I love to take pictures and have even thought about an avocation as an outdoor photographer or a traveling photographer taking black and white photographs of interesting places and interesting people. That has been my long-term goal for learning.

I have had many learning goals during my life. For a while when I was younger, it involved American Saddlebred horses. I think that they are beautiful and have dreamed of owning a few on 20 acres of land out in the country. So, I became an avid reader about American Saddlebred horses.

My learning goals have changed from time to time, but that is the fun of being a lifelong learner. You can find adventure wherever you seek it! That is one of the goals of becoming a part of this adventure that we can all share—the adventure of learning!

NOTES

1. Brett McKay and Kate McKay, "How and Why to Become a Lifelong Learner," The Art of Manliness, September 29, 2016, http://www.artofmanliness.com/2013/03/18/how-and-why-to-become-a-lifelong-learner/.

2. Edward Paxton Hood, *Self-Education: Twelve Chapters for Young Thinkers* (London: Partridge & Oakey, 1852), 12.

3. Brett and Kate McKay, "How and Why to Become a Lifelong Learner."

4. Norton Juster, *The Phantom Tollbooth* (New York: Alfred A. Knopf, 2015).

5. Michael Bond, "Success for Teens: Learning Is a Never-Ending Process," Ahwatukee Foothills News, May 27, 2014, http://www.ahwatukee.com/columns/successful_tutor/article_2c674494-a92d-11e3-bf47-0019bb2963f4.html.

6. Ravi Sankar Venna, "Why Learning Is a Continuous Process of Your Life?" SAP Blogs, September 26, 2013, https://blogs.sap.com/2013/09/26/why-learning-is-a-continuous-process-of-your-life/.

7. Ibid.

8. Deborah Jones, "A True Education Is a Never-Ending Process," Student Caring, November 16, 2014, http://studentcaring.com/true-education-never-ending-process-guest-post/.

9. Sankar Venna, "Why Learning Is a Continuous Process."

10. Bond, "Success for Teens."

11. Ibid.

12. Henry Cloud, *Never Go Back: 10 Things You'll Never Do Again* (New York: Simon & Schuster, 2015), 25.

13. Pauline Estrem, "Why Failure Is Good for Success," SUCCESS, August 25, 2016, http://www.success.com/article/why-failure-is-good-for-success.

14. Discussed in Brett and Kate McKay, "How and Why to Become a Lifelong Learner."

CHAPTER NINE

LEARNING AND TEACHING

JIM STOVALL

Learning and teaching are both part of an ongoing, upwardly spiraling cycle. I've often heard it said that the best way to really learn something is to teach it. I know that one of the most profound and enduring lessons I ever learned came out of my first attempt to be a teacher.

There are countless numbers of people to whom I owe my success. As an interviewer—both for books and columns as well as on television—I have had the privilege of meeting and interviewing some of the greatest people of the 20th and now the 21st century. These people represent the top achievers from the arenas of politics, movies, sports, and television. Many of these superstars have had a lasting impact on my life.

During publicity tours for our work on television, my new books, or the movies based on them, I am often asked by reporters which person whom I have met has impacted my life the most. I have thought a lot about it, and there is one special individual who has had a lasting impact on me. Ironically, I met him as a result of my first foray into the world of teaching.

Shortly after I learned of my impending blindness, I decided to continue with my plans to attend a local university. Near that university, there was a school for blind children, and I'm not sure if my motives were to learn more about blindness, make some kind of bargain with God, or just to help out, but in any event, I went to the school for blind children and met the principal.

I told her that I was a college freshman, and I had no background, training, or experience working with blind children, and I would like to teach in her school. You can imagine how excited she was to see me! But, she was a kind soul and told me that if I really wanted to teach there, they had one child I could work with one on one.

I agreed, and she explained that Christopher was four years old, was totally blind, and had many other physical problems. Following their many tests, they had determined that Christopher would never develop or advance any more than he already had. And what they wanted me to do was keep him quiet and keep him away from the other kids so they could learn their lessons.

As I look back on it today, I realize that Christopher was suffering from the most severe disability of all— that is, being faced with no expectations. We always live up to the expectations that we have of ourselves or those expectations that we allow other people to place upon us.

They had no expectations for Christopher, and the only training they gave me in order to work with him were two very simple things. First, they instructed me to keep his shoes tied, as they were afraid he would trip and fall because he had never learned to tie his shoelaces. Second, they told me I had to keep him away from the stairs because he had never learned to climb the stairs, and they were afraid he would fall down the staircase.

Other than those two things, they really didn't care what I did as long as I kept Christopher quiet so that the other students could learn their lessons.

That first day, I was introduced to Christopher and immediately noticed that he was, indeed, much smaller than you would expect a four-year-old child to be. He was totally blind and had many other physical problems.

He and I sat down and had a serious conversation, and I told him, "Young man, before I leave here, no matter how many weeks or months or even years it takes, you are at least going to learn how to tie your shoes and climb the stairs."

And he replied, "No, I can't."

And I responded, "Yes, you can."

And he replied, "No, I can't."

And I responded, "Yes, you can."

And he replied, "No, I can't..."

If you have ever spent any length of time with a four-year-old child, you know that they can argue like this all day long.

Christopher and I began working every day, learning how to tie his shoes and climb the stairs. Meanwhile, I was attending the university and facing what I thought were insurmountable obstacles. I couldn't see well enough to get around anymore and couldn't read the textbooks.

When it got difficult, I simply prepared to quit.

I went to the school for blind children for what I thought would be my last day. I met with the principal and told her that because of my own visual impairment and impending blindness I was going to have to drop out of college, so I wouldn't be able to come there and work with Christopher anymore because I simply couldn't make it.

I didn't realize that Christopher had been dropped off early that morning, and he was standing outside the open door to the office, hearing our entire conversation. So, as I went out to tell him goodbye and tell him that I loved him and tell him that I hoped that someday someone else would show up and spend some time with him, he turned to me and repeated my own words back at me by saying, "Yes, you can!"

And I replied, "No, I can't."

And he persisted, "Yes you can!"

And as I replied, "No, I can't" once again, I was mentally preparing an explanation so I could justify to Christopher how my challenges were somehow different or greater than his were. But, before I could begin my weak explanation, it hit me like a ton of bricks. The obvious answer was, "Stovall, either get up and do something with your life, or quit lying to this poor kid and telling him he can do things in his life."

Three years later, I graduated from that university with honors. And the same week, I had the privilege of my life, with what little vision I had left, to observe then-seven-year-old Christopher climb three flights of stairs, turn and sit on the top step, and tie both of his shoes.

About six weeks after the miraculous day when Christopher climbed the stairs and tied his shoes, he died of a brain tumor. The tumor was the condition that had caused him to lose his sight in the first place, and eventually it took his life.

As I was attending his funeral, one of the other teachers said to me, "Isn't it a shame we'll never know how much he could have developed or contributed had he been given a full life?"

I told her that he had already made his contribution, because anything I did from that point forward I would owe to him.

They tell me that I have shared Christopher's story with over a million people, live in events around the world, and now I am sharing it with you through this book. Many of those people—and hopefully you—will use Christopher's example as a platform to examine your dreams, take possession of them, remove the obstacles, eliminate the excuses, and realize that any dream you have inside of you is well within your capacity to achieve.

When Christopher died, it was almost as if he had a will. He left me three separate things that I want to pass on to you.

First, Christopher left me with the certain knowledge that there is no such thing as an insignificant person. If God had ever created an insignificant person, it would have been Christopher. His whole biography would read, "Christopher lived to be seven years old. He learned how to tie his shoes and climb the stairs." These were all of the accomplishments that Christopher could claim after his brief life, but he has changed the lives of thousands of people around the world through his example of courage.

Second, Christopher left me with the certain knowledge that there is no such thing as an insignificant relationship. All relationships are critical. Each of them is important. There are people in your world who are struggling. They're trying to decide whether their dreams can come true.

And finally, Christopher left me with the certain knowledge that there is no such thing as an insignificant day, because when we live our lives in the present, every day of the rest of our lives holds within it your key to greatness, which is your ability to build on your past and create your future by living out your destiny today, and learning valuable lessons that can be implemented in your life.

Only through teaching Christopher to tie his shoes and climb the stairs could I have ever learned the profound, impactful, and life-changing lessons he taught me, and through me and my books, columns, and speeches, he has now taught the world.

Most teachers, trainers, and professors will tell you they have received far more from their students than their students have received from them. You will have countless opportunities to teach and be taught throughout your personal and professional life. Lessons abound, and teachers come in all shapes and sizes. Most people would say that our society puts too much of a premium on sports, and we are addicted to football, basketball, baseball, and all of the other games people play.

In reality, there are approximately 850 million visits to American museums each year, more than all major league sporting events and theme parks combined. There are lectures, concerts, tours, and exhibitions available with regularity in virtually all communities, and the Internet can take you anywhere in the world you want to go and teach you the lessons that people around the world have to offer.

Life, itself, and the examples people provide us may be the most masterful teacher of all. For many years, I have traveled to San Diego for regular meetings and speaking engagements. On my first visit, I met a cab driver named Ali who had just come to America as a refugee from Somalia. I made arrangements for him to pick me up on my next trip, and we continued this process over many years. Ali barely knew our language when he came to America, but in addition to the incredibly long hours he worked, he went to night school and read voraciously. Eventually, he compiled enough money to bring his wife and children to America and was able to pay for all the legal fees associated with him and his family becoming American citizens.

He and I had long conversations as we traversed the congested California freeways during each of my trips. He told me of all the progress he was making in his personal and professional life as time went by. Eventually, he no longer worked as an employee for the cab company but bought his own car and started a sedan and limousine service. Over time, he acquired a second car, then a third car, and I long ago lost count of how many vehicles his company owns and operates.

During one of my more recent trips, Ali told me he wanted to take a slight detour to buy gas. When I asked why he didn't want to stop at one of the gas stations right on the freeway, he told me he preferred to use the gas station he owned.

I remember asking Ali how he came from being an uneducated, illiterate Somalian refugee and became a well-respected, wealthy American businessman. He chuckled wisely and said, "Mr. Stovall, I learned it from you and businesspeople like you. I couldn't always go to school or even read, but I was always able to watch and learn."

There are teachers all around you where you live and work right now. They are ready, willing, and able to teach you profound and life-changing lessons if you will just be open to learning. School is always in session. Be sure you're paying attention and taking notes.

CHAPTER TEN

COGNITION AS THE BASIS FOR LEARNING: HOW DO WE LEARN?

RAY H. HULL, PHD

LET'S FIRST DEFINE "COGNITION"

The term *cognition* is sometimes confused with the concept of "being aware," as in, "She seems to be cognizant of what is going on around her." Well, that is close to being correct, but not quite. When we talk about the term *cognition*, the true definition refers to the mental action of acquiring knowledge and understanding and using it constructively. It encompasses such mental processes as knowledge acquisition, memory, judgment, reasoning, problem-solving, decision-making, and computation.

When I think of "cognition" and cognitive changes that frequently accompany the process of aging, I equate those changes with the ability to use one's existing knowledge to generate or gain new knowledge. In other words, the ability to use what one has learned throughout one's life in the decision-making process—for example, making quick decisions that are on target, going to the bank and engaging in accurate money transactions, creative and constructive thinking when buying a new car, drawing upon what we have learned, mentally organizing it in a logical manner, and presenting it before an audience.

Another way of looking at cognition is by thinking in terms of information processing—the mental processing of information and the ability to use it with agility and flexibility. An example of that is being able to engage in a debate by drawing on information that one person has stored in their brain that can be used to counter the argument of the other person or to reach an agreement by bringing both sides of an argument into harmony with each other using constructive and creative reasoning.

USING WHAT WE LEARN

Cognition refers to using what we learn in what we do in our lives. When we learn new information on a certain subject, and if it is something that can be used in our work, our everyday life, or our recreational life, we take that information, organize those aspects that can be utilized to our benefit, and then apply them in such a way that they can enhance that aspect of our life. That means taking what we have learned and using it constructively to benefit us in our life or our work, or for the benefit others.

Jean Piaget was one of the most influential researchers in the field of cognitive development. He studied his own three children as they developed from infancy to early adulthood, and through those and other observations developed his "theory of cognitive development." He believed that human development was different from what is found in animals because humans develop the capacity to engage in abstract symbolic reasoning.

The stages that he observed in children as they moved through cognitive development from infancy into early adulthood are as follows:[1]

Infancy, Ages 0–2 Years

There is motor activity, but no language symbols. Basic knowledge is developing that at this time is limited. Developing knowledge is based on immediate experiences and interactions with non-animate objects and figures and humans. The mobility of the child allows for her or him to learn new things. Some language skills are developed throughout this period but are primarily receptive in nature, with increasing skill in expressive language throughout. The child is learning basic cognitive knowledge of time, space, and cause and effect.

Toddler and Early Childhood, Ages 2–7 Years

This a broad span of development! From age two to age seven involves incredible advances in a child's cognitive development. The brain is expanding tremendously in its capacity to acquire basic knowledge, both receptive and expressive language, visual and auditory recognition and cognition, motor development—from walking and running and on to elementary school track meets and more. It must have been difficult for Piaget to present his developmental findings for this span of ages as so much is happening during those five years.

But, even though I am sure with some difficulty, Piaget describes what he discovered through his observations for this span of ages. For example, memory and imagination are definitely maturing during this period of development; the child develops intuitive problem solving (revealing expansive cognitive development), the ability to see relationships, and the ability to read fluently during those years; self-concept is developing although somewhat fragile during this time; and language is developing in ever increasing complexity.

Elementary Grades and Early Adolescence, Ages 7–12 Years

Again, this is a very broad expanse of mental and physical development, that is, from about the second or third grade in elementary school to seventh or eighth grade in intermediate or middle school. So much occurs during those years in relation to expanded language development, development of knowledge of math concepts including those of basic algebra, vocabulary development as they relate to numerous academic subjects, motor development including refined coordination and running speed, expanded precision in hand-eye coordination, and many others. And so it must have been difficult to include this span of ages in a systematic description of child development.

So again, here is Piaget's description of cognitive development for the ages of seven through early adolescence:

The child is able to think in more complex ways, for example, "What would happen if the reverse was true?" The child is able to accept the role of another person and act on it. She or he develops the ability to understand the concepts of mass, volume, and weight. Egocentric thinking is clearly evident, manipulation of language and language concepts is intact but still expanding, the intelligence of the child is becoming clearly evident not only in regard to test scores but the child's ability to communicate utilizing complex thought processes that will impress adults who are present and listening.

Adolescence and Adulthood, Age 12 Years and Beyond

Cognitive development continues to expand throughout one's life from adolescence through adulthood. Abstract thinking has expanded and will continue to expand throughout one's life. Complex reasoning and problem-solving has developed and will continue to develop. In adolescence, adults are generally impressed with young people's ability to problem-solve, thinking that those abilities are beyond what they should be at that age. Learning will continue throughout the individual's life, and such mental gymnastics as are required for flexibility in thought processes, and the use of complex reasoning skills will likewise continue to develop.

HOW DO WE LEARN?

How do we learn? What cognitive processes are activated that cause learning to take place? In accessing UNESCO's International Institute for Educational Planning, the following was discovered that an overview of research on learning involves many dimensions, including neurological, physical, social, emotional, and more:

The processes involved in learning depend to some extent on what is being learned: a new word and the concept behind it, a physical skill or a mental skill, an attitude, a habit, appropriate social etiquette, or more. But most objects of learning are complex and involve many of these aspects simultaneously—new mental connections and new ways of thinking, new ways of using the body to accomplish a task, learning how to execute some tasks automatically or habitually to leave space for more complex mental demands.[2]

There are so many mental, physical, environmental, and social variables that impact on the process of learning that it is mind-boggling, to say the least. Anthropology, cognitive science, computer science, neuroscience, psychology, sociology, and many other fields are all involved in the study of learning. Every new theory of learning brings about more controversy regarding how we learn, what is involved in the process of learning, how learning takes place within various environments, and so on. I was reading an article the other day that attempted to debunk all of the previous theories of learning that have evolved over the past several centuries by saying that they are all wrong, that, for example, learning has nothing to do with nurture or the child's environment, social climate, when education begins in a child's life, the best environment for studying, and so on. The author was suggesting that research on the process of learning begin all over again.

Perhaps an article written by the editors of *Scientific American* gives us a peek into the confusion that confronts us when we study the process of learning and attempt to assimilate the vast number of theories of learning that have evolved over the years. They state, "When we pack our children off to school for the first time, we envision them embarking on a lifelong career of learning. Yet one thing they typically never study is the art of studying itself."[3] It is assumed that learning will take place whether the child wants to learn or not. Yet, there are variables to learning that we often times don't think to consider. For example, children frequently are not taught the art of studying, the art of exploration, the art of questioning the processes that teachers utilize in teaching, the joy of lifelong learning, or the art of handwriting, which assists students greatly in the process of studying rather than only using a computer, digital tablet, or iPad keyboard.

Children learn in many different ways. For example, in the IIEP Learning Portal they describe a child who accompanies a parent to the grocery store. Whether these learning components are discussed or not, the child is learning about the use of arithmetic, financial aspects of a marketplace, the economy, and the many items and compartments that make up a complete store that is based on selling to the public. However, think of how much more the child would learn if the child's parent would talk about the store and its components, how much each item costs within the realm of the cash that the parent has available, the nutritional value of the various fruits and vegetables that are being placed in the grocery cart, and so on.[4]

LEARNING, COGNITION, AND THE IMPACT OF MEMORY

According to John Kihlstrom in a presentation at the University of California, Berkeley on the topic of learning, he describes it as "a relatively permanent change in knowledge that occurs as a result of experience. That knowledge is reflected in the organism's behavior, but the important thing is that learning changes the individual's fund of knowledge."[5] Thus, by virtue of learning, knowledge becomes available for later use once it is stored in the individual's memory. That is an interesting definition of learning, but it really doesn't tell us very much.

Learning, of course, requires memory—essentially *storage for recall* to be used when important. But, there are a number of forms of memory that are used in learning. In turn, knowledge that requires *long-term memory*, or long-term storage-for-recall, is the principal form of memory that we talk about when attempting to describe the process of "learning." For example, long-term memory stores *declarative knowledge*, which is factual knowledge about what is true and what is false, and long-term memory stores *procedural knowledge*—knowledge of skills and rules or how to do things. Kihlstrom describes these two types of knowledge:

> There are two kinds of **procedural knowledge**: **motor procedures**, like how to shift gears in a standard-shift car, and **mental procedures**, like how to calculate square roots.
>
> And there are two kinds of **declarative knowledge**: **episodic knowledge** is essentially autobiographical memory, for particular events that have a unique location in space and time; **semantic knowledge** is more abstract, like a mental dictionary or encyclopedia.[6]

For an example of semantic knowledge, I remember the twelve major cranial nerves that I learned in my basic neurology course by recalling the mnemonic, "On old Olympus' towering tops, a Fin and German viewed some hops'" which reminds me of each of the twelve major cranial nerves—*optic, olfactory, oculomotor, tragus, trigeminal*, and so on and so on. They are recorded in the neuronal storage banks of my brain somewhere between my working memory and my long-term memory.

Even though learning involves both decoding of information (to convert a code into usable language) and encoding (converting language into a code that we can use), we primarily use *encoding*—a process by which new information is placed into memory, that information is stored in our central nervous system, and we can retrieve that information and use it. The most efficient form of encoding is what is called *elaborative rehearsal,* which involves connecting something that we are trying to learn and remember with something that we already know. For example, we tend to remember a person's name whom we just met if we perchance realize that she looks just like another person we have known for some time who has a similar name. Or, we will tend to remember the name of the explorer we learned about in grade school who had the same first name as our grandfather. In other words, we are connecting the new item with our rich bank of pre-existing knowledge.

"So here's the first key to learning: we learn best when we learn progressively, building new knowledge on old knowledge."[7] This seems very logical, and it makes absolute sense! When I think back to my country school days, I remembered my history and geography lessons best when I could apply the information to our life on our farm or the stories that my grandfather had previously told me about his young life in Wales. I remembered that information perfectly at examination time! For other information that I was required to learn, I had to either memorize or try desperately to relate it to something that I already knew, which didn't always work.

We also learn things best when we determine how they relate to other things, how they link together, rather than learning each item individually. In addition, Kihlstrom stresses:

> Perhaps for the same reason, Oppenheimer and Mueller (2014) found that handwritten class notes yield better recall of lecture material than notes taken on a laptop. It takes more effort to write than to type, and the additional effort apparently produces a richer, more memorable memory trace. All of which is just one more reason to lament the tendency, in current elementary education, to de-emphasize cursive in favor of printing or even (God help those students) keyboarding.[8]

THE IMPACT OF OUR EMOTIONAL STATE ON LEARNING

Mark Barajas stresses a further observation on enhanced functioning of cognitive skills and learning. He emphasizes the positive affect of "mild positive emotional states on a wide range of human behavior and cognitive processes."[8]

The author states that positive feelings, no matter what the source, have been shown to enhance one's ability to problem-solve, be more creative, and function in a freer frame of mind as opposed to attempting to function mentally when in a negative frame of mind. Developing problem-solving strategies that are more creative in nature appears to be the result of a positive outlook on the part of the problem solver.

When one is in a happy frame of mind, the problem solver is more apt to gain access to information that she or he has stored in their central nervous system. They therefore have the ability to make use of a wider range of creative ideas and a wider range of information for the development of those ideas.

So, according to Barajas, "For educators, being mindful of creating and maintaining a warm, positive classroom environment may enhance students' ability to creatively problem solve."[9] The same can be suggested for physicians, dentists, and others who may find patients or clients feeling uncomfortable about being there when discussing possible approaches to serving their needs.

PERHAPS LEARNING IS NOT AS SIMPLE AND STRAIGHTFORWARD AS ONCE THOUGHT

Annie Murphy Paul has written an interesting treatise on the fact that learning may not be as simple and obvious as researchers once proposed:

> Parents, teachers, and other experts are full of sensible-sounding advice about how to learn well: select a particular place to study and use it consistently; concentrate on one subject at a time; focus intensively on the

material just before a test or an important meeting.[10]

But, according to Paul, "It turns out that learning is not so simple and obvious."[11] She continues by saying that the tools of neuroscience and cognitive psychology have uncovered something that reverses our former thinking about the process of learning. That is, "The brain has its own set of rules by which it learns best."[12] And every brain has a different set of rules. Therefore, everyone learns differently. This has been obvious for centuries, but teacher training institutions have traditionally prepared educators to believe that every child and every adult learns by the same set of rules. So, classrooms and assignments given to students assume that students all learn in the same way.

That is an unfortunate set of circumstances for learners of all ages. They are not given an opportunity to learn in their own way, thus allowing many to not do as well as they otherwise might have. Guidance by a teacher is important, but the teacher should not force students to learn in one regimented way. It simply doesn't work.

THERE ARE MANY LEVELS OF LEARNING

There are many levels of learning and many avenues that lead to learning, not just one. According to UNESCO, "Simple skills often need to be mastered before moving on to more difficult ones. But the ultimate goal of learning is to become capable of purposefully generating novel solutions and further learning in new contexts."[13] It is important to develop what is called "adaptive expertise"—"the ability to apply meaningfully-learned knowledge and skills flexibly and creatively in different situations." Simply put:

> The development of adaptive expertise [which should be the goal of all educational environments] depends on five components: 1) a well-organized knowledge base, 2) strategies for problem analysis and transformation, 3) meta-knowledge [underlying factors] about one's own thinking and emotions, 4) self-regulatory skills [controlling our own emotions and ability to stick to tasks and complete them], and 5) positive beliefs about oneself, the subject, and the context. In other words, the goal of learning is not only to develop knowledge [which is the primary goal taught to many teachers-in-training in university departments of education], but also the thinking strategies and the emotional understanding and skills necessary to use them—whether in routine or novel contexts.[14]

SO, WHAT IS LEARNING?

In reviewing all that I have written in this section of this chapter, what exactly is involved in learning?

It *requires memory*, both short-term and long-term memory. In particular, long-term memory, which is responsible for both storage of information for the long term and recall, including:

1. Factual knowledge—knowledge of skills and rules

2. Episodic knowledge—autobiographical memory for people and specific events that have a special place in a person's life

3. Procedural knowledge—including motor procedures, or how to do things manually, and mental procedures such as solving math problems

4. Semantic knowledge—our mental dictionary or encyclopedia of words, facts, and events, among others

It *requires both decoding* (converting a code into usable language) *and encoding* (converting language into a code that we can use). We primarily use encoding in the process of learning as we place new information into memory. The most efficient form of encoding involves *elaborative rehearsal*—connecting something that we are trying to learn with something we already know.

Learning involves the impact of one's *emotional state*. A positive emotional state affects a wide range of human behavior and cognitive processes. Research shows that memory and learning are enhanced when learners are in a positive state of mind.

Learning may not be as simple and obvious as researchers once proposed. Departments of education in universities have typically taught that every child and every adult learns by the same set of rules—that they all learn in the same way—but this goes against what neuroscience and cognitive psychology have uncovered. The brain has its own set of rules for learning, and every child and every adult learns differently!

The *goal of learning* is not only to develop knowledge, but also to develop thinking strategies and the emotional understanding and skills necessary to use those strategies.

NOTES

1. Jean Piaget, *The Origins of Intelligence in Children* (Madison, CT: International Universities Press, 1974).

2. International Institute for Educational Planning, "How Do We Learn?" IIEP Learning Portal, accessed July 09, 2017, https://learningportal.iiep. unesco.org/en/how-we-learn.

3. The Editors, "How We Learn," Scientific American, September 1, 2013, https://www .scientificamerican.com/article/how-we-learn/.

4. IIEP Learning Portal, "How Do We Learn?" The Social Dimension of Learning.

5. John F. Kihlstrom, *How Students Learn—And How We Can Help Them*, University of California, Berkeley, Department of Psychology, January 17, 2017, http://socrates.berkeley.edu/~kihlstrm/GSI_2011.htm.

6. Ibid.

7. Ibid.

8. Mark S. Barajas, "Thinking And Feeling: The Influence of Positive Emotion on Human Cognition," *The Hilltop Review*, 3rd ser., 7, no. 1, pg. 4 (December 2014), http://scholarworks.wmich.edu/cgi/viewcontent.cgi?article=1084&context=hilltopreview.

9   Ibid., 10.

10. Annie Murphy Paul, "The Real Learning Curve," Time, October 12, 2011, http://ideas.time.com/2011/10/12/the-science-of-how-we-learn/.

11 Ibid.

12. Ibid.

13. IIEP Learning Portal, "How Do We Learn?" The Goal of Learning: Adaptive Expertise.

14. E. de Corte, qtd. in IIEP Learning Portal, "How Do We Learn?"

CHAPTER ELEVEN

LEARNING RECAP

JIM STOVALL

If you were familiar with my work at all prior to reading this book, it's probably because of a bestselling novel I wrote and the major motion picture based on it entitled *The Ultimate Gift*. *The Ultimate Gift* is a story that eventually stretched over four novels and a movie trilogy. It recounts the exploits of a self-made billionaire named Red Stevens masterfully portrayed in the film by James Garner.

As the story goes, near the end of his life Red Stevens realizes that although he's made billions of dollars and conquered the world in his business career, he has failed pitifully as a family man. In an attempt to rectify this shortcoming, Red Stevens drafts his will in such a way that his grandson Jason will not become an instant millionaire but, instead, will be confronted with a series of 12 monthly tasks or quests that Red Stevens labels as gifts.

Only if Jason adequately performs everything required in each of the gifts will he receive his inheritance. Jason goes through the gift of money, the gift of work, the gifts of friends, family, love, and several others, but among the most profound gift Jason receives from his grandfather Red Stevens is the gift of learning.

In this gift, Jason Stevens—who has been raised as a wealthy, privileged young man who never wanted for anything—is required to travel to an impoverished, remote, mountainous area in Central America. There, through prearrangement, he encounters a village where he is required to work for an entire month in the library.

Jason had lived his whole life in close proximity to a number of world-renowned libraries that he had never visited, so he didn't know what to expect when he entered the dilapidated, ramshackle library hut in Central America.

As he entered the facility, he was struck by the fact that it had a dirt floor, a few dusty shelves, and almost no books. When he inquired about the dearth of books, the pleasant and energetic librarian told him excitedly that the books were out with all the people. She informed Jason that books don't do any good sitting on the shelf.

Jason, who had been given all the opportunities to take advantage of every educational privilege, learned during his month in the jungle about the passion, pleasure, and benefits people can derive from the gift of learning.

All learning builds on previous learning and becomes the basis for even more learning in the future. My hope is that this book will become the springboard for you to make learning a constant companion and an integral part of the rest of your life.

As with all of my other books, I don't simply want to be a writer; instead, I want to be your partner in learning from this moment forward.

Any time your dreams, goals, or aspirations seem to be too far away and impossible to reach, or any time you simply need to reevaluate and fine-tune your learning, I can be reached at 918-627-1000 or Jim@JimStovall.com.

Learning, as Red Stevens taught his grandson, is a gift. It is a gift that enhances the lives of both the teacher and the student. If you learn more, you will grow. And if you share that which you have learned with others, you will change the lives of countless people including yourself.

ABOUT
JIM STOVALL

In spite of blindness, Jim Stovall has been a National Olympic weightlifting champion, a successful investment broker, the president of the Emmy Award-winning Narrative Television Network, and a highly sought-after author and platform speaker. He is the author of 40 books including the bestseller *The Ultimate Gift*, which is now a major motion picture from 20th Century Fox starring Games Garner and Abigail Breslin. Five of his other novels have also been made into movies with two more in production.

Steve Forbes, president and CEO of *Forbes* magazine, says, "Jim Stovall is one of the most extraordinary men of our era."

For his work in making television accessible to our nation's 13 million blind and visually impaired people, the President's Committee on Equal Opportunity selected Jim Stovall as the Entrepreneur of the Year. Jim Stovall has been featured in *The Wall Street Journal*, *Forbes* magazine, *USA Today*, and has been seen on *Good Morning America*, *CNN*, and *CBS Evening News*. He was also chosen as the International Humanitarian of the Year, joining Jimmy Carter, Nancy Reagan, and Mother Teresa as recipients of this honor.

Jim Stovall can be reached at 918-627-1000 or Jim@JimStovall.com.

ABOUT
RAY H. HULL, PH.D.

Raymond H. Hull, PhD, FASHA, FAAA is Professor of Communication Sciences and Disorders, College of Health Professions, Wichita State University. He was Chair of the Department of Communication Disorders, University of Northern Colorado for twelve years and during that time was also Director of Planning and Budget for the Office of the President for seven successful years. He held administrative posts within the graduate school, being responsible for graduate program review at the University of Northern Colorado for ten years and Wichita State University for eight years.

Background: His background in the fields of communication and the neuroscience of human communication began with his BA degree in public speaking, drama, and radio/television broadcast, and then moved into graduate work in disorders of human communication at the graduate level, and then a doctorate in the neuroscience of human communication that involved a combined doctoral degree from the University of Denver and University of Colorado School of Medicine. He works extensively in coaching and speaking on "The Art of Interpersonal Communication in Professional Life"—in other words, the nature of interpersonal communication that supports success in one's professional life.

He is sought after as a speaker/presenter in the U.S. and other countries and has authored and presented over 600 presentations and workshops across the U.S., Canada, South America, and Europe mostly on the art of communication in professional practice, environmental design for communication, and central auditory processing in children and the older adults. He has written and published 18 books in the field of communication, public speaking, and communication sciences and disorders. His book entitled *The Art of Communication*, which was co-authored with New York Times Best Selling Author Jim Stovall, was published in 2016 by Sound Wisdom Publishing. *The Art of Presentation* was also co-authored with Jim Stovall and published early 2017. Another new book authored and edited by Ray Hull entitled *Communication Disorders in Aging*, published by Plural Publishing, was released in spring, 2017.

Dr. Hull is the recipient of numerous honors and awards. He was named Distinguished Pioneer in Gerontology by the Colorado Gerontological Society. He was awarded the Public Health Service Award, U.S. Public Health Service, PHS for significant service to United States Public Health Service for research and service on behalf of hearing-impaired older adults. He was awarded the Red River Award by the Manitoba Ministry of Health and the Winnipeg League for the Hard of Hearing, Winnipeg, Manitoba, for significant service on behalf of hearing-impaired adults. He has also been named Distinguished University Scholar, University of Northern Colorado, twice named College Scholar, College of Health and Human Sciences, University of Northern Colorado, the Delores and Sydney Rodenberg Award for Teaching Excellence, Wichita State University, and many other awards and honors. He is Fellow of the American Speech-Language-Hearing Association and Fellow of the American Academy of Audiology.

TO CLAIM YOUR ADDITIONAL FREE RESOURCES PLEASE VISIT

JIMSTOVALLBOOKS.COM

If you enjoyed this book, try these other

JIM STOVALL BOOKS

Wisdom for Winners Vol. 1	Ultimate Hindsight
Wisdom for Winners Vol. 2	Wisdom of the Ages
The Millionaire Map	Success Secrets of Super Achievers
The Ultimate Gift	You Don't Have to be Blind to See
The Ultimate Life	The Art of Communication
The Ultimate Journey	The Art of Presentation
The Ultimate Legacy	The Art of Productivity
The Gift of a Legacy	The Lamp
The Ultimate Financial Plan	Discovering Joye
Ultimate Productivity	A Christmas Snow

AVAILABLE EVERYWHERE BOOKS ARE SOLD

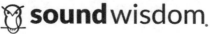